The Monsters Are Here

Stories by

Lori D'Angelo

Copyright © 2024 Lori D'Angelo

All rights reserved. No part of this publication may be reproduced, distributed, or transmitted in any form or by any means, including photocopying, recording, or other electronic or mechanical methods, without the prior written permission of the publisher, except in the case of brief quotations embodied in critical reviews and certain other noncommercial uses permitted by copyright law. For permission requests, write to the publisher at the address below.

ELJ Editions, Ltd. is committed to publishing works of quality and integrity. In that spirit, we are proud to offer this story collection to our readers. This is a work of fiction. Names, characters, places, and incidents either are the product of the author's imagination or are used fictitiously, and any resemblance to actual persons, living or dead, business establishments, events, or locales is entirely coincidental.

ISBN: 978-1-942004-78-3

Library of Congress Control Number: 2024945001

Cover Design by ELJ Editions, Ltd.
Author Photo by Christa Good

ELJ Editions, Ltd.
P.O. Box 815
Washingtonville, NY 10992

www.elj-editions.com

Praise for The Monsters Are Here

You'd better strap in because Lori D'Angelo is taking you places. A little bit of Kelly Link, a little Kathy Fish, D'Angelo is most of all herself, bringing us the most imaginative collection of fiction I have had the pleasure of reading in a long time. *The Monsters Are Here* heralds a new voice in contemporary fiction—I can't wait to see what Lori D'Angelo does next.

—Stephanie Vanderslice, author of *The Lost Son and The Geek's Guide to the Writing Life*

Monsters are here. So are vampires, mermaids, murderers, werewolves, fortunetellers, and dozens of less outlandish but no less remarkable characters. Lori D'Angelo's debut collection is as entertaining as it is unpredictable. Each story is a ride into the strange and stunning. Read this book, and you'll be dazed, dazzled, and delighted.

—Mark Brazaitis, author of *American Seasons and The Incurables*

The monsters are here, and what a glorious invasion it is! Whether it's an uptight vampire accountant stretching her fangs or a werewolf realizing she loves her dad-boded buddy, the characters in Lori D'Angelo's debut story collection are wonderfully human. These, smart, often hilarious tales haunted me in the best possible way.

—Shari Goldhagen, author of *In Some Other World, Maybe*

What an exciting debut for Lori D'Angelo with her collection, *The Monsters Are Here*. Each of these stories introduces a new spectacle of innovation and heart, of humor and horror. D'Angelo's characters occupy worlds where the impossible overlaps the real and sincerity is bordered by absurdity. I loved reading these stories, eating them up one after another, so engrossed by these narratives, this writer's vision.

—Michael Czyzniejewski, author of *The Amnesiac in the Maze: Stories*

For My Family,

Including all the four-legged members who have passed through our lives and touched our hearts

Contents

The Monsters Are Here	3
Street Show Magic	7
The Good Wolf	10
The Girl in the Mirror	20
The Vampire Accountant	21
Hot Dog from Heaven	26
Outside Eden	30
The Expert Consultant from Amityville Gives Her Opinion on Your Second-Rate	44
The Other Elizabeth	46
Belonging	59
Ohio River Oracle	61
Water, Power, Danger	78
The Great Escape	80
Close to You	89
What Remains	91
Life Me Up, Drag Me Down	102
A Tale of Two Cats	104
Basically, Don't	110
Searching for the Dead	112

The Cold Zone	120
Mirror, Mirror	123
How It Happened	128
The Fortune Teller	130
Under the Knife	140
The Fixer	143
Hunger	156
Secrets	159
I'm Not Karen	165
The Man I Loved, The Man I Married	172
Just Like Home	181

The Monsters Are Here

We called the man Frankenstein after the novel, like that was normal. Like it was okay to mock the disabled and deformed. There were so many bone-chilling incidents I could tell you about. But I'll only share a few.

Like how we saw him at the Olive Garden and laughed at him trying to slurp down his unlimited soup and shovel in breadsticks with his shaky ice-cream scooper-like hands. We posted a video about it on TikTok. It got 52,000 likes.

One among us tried to stop it. But we threw him in a pit with the others. In our defense, we didn't exactly kill the irritating whistleblower wannabee. But he was most likely dead. It's hard to breathe in pits once you are covered by dirt. We didn't confirm because we weren't going to stick around for the Edgar Allen Poe aftermath.

As my grandpa always used to say, "Snitches get stitches." I never asked him to clarify if he ever saw this really happen. And, if so, who was the one sewing in the stitches? And did anyone ever take them out?

It was too late to ask Grandpa now. He had already been dragged through the gates of Hell and was living unhappily down under. And all my letters got marked return to sender before they spontaneously burst into flames. I had to hand it to them. It was an efficient means of disposing of unwanted fan mail. It wasn't like that time I worked for that guy who had been an extra in that iconic John Hughes movie whose requests for appearances piled up until he finally got so mad that he sent them crashing through the garage window like Ferris Bueller's friend Cameron's car.

With the Piggy figure among us gone, we suspected that the girl with the cleft palate wanted to protest our awfulness because, even after her face-fixing surgery, she never really looked pretty enough to get catcalled on that horrifying stretch of road between the *we will pray for you* clinic and the upscale coffee shop, which was only three city blocks and five light years apart. It was that area of the city where the rest of us braced for impact because we love/hated to have our bodies objectified. It made us realize that while we were mostly only valued for our looks, we, as women, weren't dried up disposable yet. But she kept her not-quite-regular mouth shut, and we let her exist on the periphery of popular because she had a car, and, sometimes, we needed a ride to the ATM, and she never made us pay for gas.

We didn't just ostracize him when we saw him. We also went out of our way to make his away-from-otherpeople-time as terrible as possible. One weekend, we decorated his yard with 360 *Wish You Were Dead* placards. In our defense, who can resist a buy two, get one free discount outlet sale?

And, as if that weren't enough, we covered his nicer-than-we-could-afford luxury sedan in fake puke that we got from the gag gift store at the nearly dead mall. Most of the good stores at that mall had closed six years ago, but somehow it still managed to stay open with just a GameStop, a Bath & Body Works, a Chick-Fil-A, an all-you-can-eat buffet, an eyebrow threading place, the puke shop, and Belk as the anchor store. It just goes to show that even Hell probably has chain store–filled shopping malls that stock all the items you could and should live without but choose not to because who doesn't feel the need to stock up on hand sanitizer and horror games?

Keith, the unofficial leader of our hate group, was not so secretly hoping that the man would leave town. His last campaign to drive out migrant workers had been so successful that the poultry processing plants in town were so understaffed now that every other week it seemed like someone lost a finger or a hand. Keith's own brother, who had only graduated high school because the vice principal took pity on him and let him pass developmental English when he could barely read, was down to seven fingers. An immigrant from Cuba who Keith called Juan because Keith said *aren't they all the same* helped his brother pass math. Keith made sure that Juan, whose real name was Oscar, was on the first bus out. Keith's brother no longer spoke to him. Sometimes, when Keith was drunk on Rebel Yell Whiskey, he called his brother and cried. But Keith's calls went straight to voicemail. None of us could blame Keith's brother for cutting him off. Oscar was his brother's best friend. My sister, Mel, who also worked at the plant but still had all her fingers so far, said that Keith's brother kept in touch with Oscar. She also said that Oscar had won a scholarship contest and attended college now. Oscar was trying to find Keith's brother a safer job at an Amazon distribution center up near where he lived. We all knew that if Keith's brother had the chance to leave, he would.

Maybe there was no defending us, but we didn't know then that the man's father had invented those phone holder things that everyone owns now, and that the man had moved down here because he had read on one of those lie after lie websites promoted by the Normalsville Chamber of Commerce that our town was a nice place to live. We only found that out after, when we realized that, though unattractive, he was a person after all.

One day, we woke up, and the man was gone without a trace. No forwarding address. No car, no furniture. Just a brochure showing people in our town looking caring and welcoming while idyllic citizens decorated the Christmas tree near the ice rink with a link to the Chamber of Commerce website, which, after that, appeared to be permanently down. The real estate company tried to sell the man's house. But no one wanted to buy it. Most likely, it would just be converted to cheap shoddy student housing like most everything else.

Keith thinks that the man moved somewhere else like Keith's brother planned to. But the move was just too quiet and too quick. No one saw or heard a thing. After that, our hate group disbanded. Because, with the man who was not a monster gone, we had nothing to keep us together. Now I sometimes hang out with the girl who had the semi-successful face surgery. She seems to know that I'm hesitant to be seen with her in public. So we drive two towns over to Rin Tin's Pin's Bowling Alley just about every other Friday night.

I think now that the monster-seeming man was sent by God to test us. And we failed so bad. Like the man on the street corner by the half dead mall says, "Vengeance is coming." I don't doubt that.

Part of me wants to drive out to the pit and climb in and see if I'll catch fire and disappear like the letters I sent to Grandpa did. Nonexistence would be a relief. But I know that's more than I deserve.

Street Show Magic

We weren't the first in line, but we also weren't the last. We, like everyone else in town, had seen the flyers, and we wanted to experience the magic.

The flyers said *Boy who can turn rocks into precious gems*, but we didn't quite believe them.

If that were the case, then why wasn't the boy living in a mansion somewhere sipping all the chocolate milk he could drink, endlessly dunking Oreos, and watching *Cartoon Network* on an endless loop?

If that were the case, then why did we have to find out about the attraction on plain old paper, instead of in a modern way like on the television or the Internet where everything that was legitimate (and many things that weren't) became true?

Like, without the Internet, we wouldn't know if a well-known actress who had once been important by association and gone on a bender was dead, sort of dead, or really dead this time.

Things had to be said and confirmed and then verified for us to believe them (though we believed things of questionable veracity all the time). *Eat more Spinach, live to 100. Do crossword puzzles, prevent Alzheimer's. Practice yoga five times a week, lower your blood pressure.*

I think we would have believed it more if an influencer had uploaded a video about it on TikTok. But the signs said, *no video recordings of any kind*, and, because they used a scary Gothic font, people listened.

The group in front of us came out of the tent shaking their heads, and I couldn't tell if that was good or bad. No one seemed to ask, and no one seemed to tell.

None of us wanted to be like the asshole on Twitter who ruins the Marvel movie for everyone else.

They let in five people at a time, and, somehow, by some weird mathematical abnormality, my party was split into two.

In one group was Mom and Tim. In the other group was me.

"See you outside, Jenny," they said.

"Yeah," I said though I was a little intimidated to be experiencing the spectacle solo.

When it was my turn, we went into the tent all hush hush, as if we were entering a holy place.

"Greetings," the boy said mechanically, as if he were a TV show alien.

Live long and prosper, I was tempted to say back.

But, instead, we just stared at each other until the boy's handler asked, "Does anyone have a rock?"

Ever the Girl Scout, I reached into my pocket. "I do! I do!" I said in my best teacher's pet voice. In fact, I had five, in case some were defective or in case we could get the boy to do a two-for-one kind of deal.

The handler took the rock, and I watched carefully, to make sure that he didn't do some sleight of hand switcheroo. The boy held the rock for a moment and then looked deep into my eyes. When the handler gave the rock back, it was my rock but not my rock. It was topaz or garnet or some other obscure birthstone gem. I had questions like, *could he make diamonds on demand, and did he do birthday parties?* I felt energized, excited, eager to talk about what happened with Mom and Tim.

But when I found them, Mom was eating peanut butter crackers that she got out of her fanny pack, and Tim was drinking a Coke that he had conned Mom into buying from a nearby food truck.

I waited for someone to speak. Finally, Tim said confidently, "Well, that was a bust."

"Yeah," I said because I was used to being agreeable. "Can I get a hot dog?"

Mom fished out five sweaty ones from her fanny pack and handed them over.

Once at the hot dog stand, I asked the hairy-armed vendor if he thought this whole sideshow was legit.

He shrugged then said, "Doesn't matter. Either way, it's good for business."

While I waited for him to slather on mustard and onions to make the hot dog perfect, I put my hand into my pocket, fumbling for the gem, in order to confirm the real was real.

The Good Wolf

They told Laura not to go to the forest. But she went anyway. She was never one to take other people's advice. Especially when the advice was meant to limit her movement, box her in.

"You know what they say about women alone in the forest?" her friend Jack asked her.

"No," she said. Because she really didn't. She expected that it was some kind of *Little Red Riding Hood* lame.

Jack laughed. "Neither do I," he admitted. "But I think it's supposed to be dangerous."

"More dangerous than a woman alone in a parking garage, a woman alone in dark alley, a woman sleeping alone in her bed at night?"

"Probably not," Jack admitted.

"If you're so worried about me, you could come," Laura said as she stuffed a waterproof blanket into her heavy-duty backpack. She also had five days' worth of MREs, a Camelback, a water filter, a lightweight chair, a paper map, a first aid kit, a compass, and a bunch of other stuff she might or might not need.

"But you're walking, right?" Jack said, as he patted his not so cute anymore gut. "Truthfully," he said, "I'm not in shape for that right now."

"What are you talking about? You look great."

"Oh, you know you're such a liar," he said. "But, as promised, I'll give you a ride to the trailhead."

They pulled into the parking lot, and Jack looked at the weather map on his smartphone with concern. "Laura, it's supposed to storm."

"I have this waterproof parka," she said lightly. "I'll be

fine. I mean I get to experience nature in all its raw beauty. I should be worried about you, boxed into your city cell, divorced from the elements."

"You know there's no shame in," Jack began.

"I've been planning this trip ever since Rob left," Laura said. "It's the only thing that's been keeping me sane."

"I know," he said. "I'm sorry. It's just that I worry about you," he said, gently putting his hand to her wrist, her scars.

"Jack, I'm okay, really," she said. "And I'll be just fine alone " Laura flexed her muscles to show him. She was brave. She was strong. She was ready for this.

He reached over to give her a kiss. She assumed it would be a peck on the cheek for luck, the kind of *hey we're friends who care about each* kiss they usually exchanged. But perhaps the forest made him bold because he kissed her firmly on the lips with quite a bit of tongue, a kiss she did not anticipate, but she liked it. "Hmm, wow," she said. "That was a surprise."

"A good one, I hope," he said.

She didn't respond. Instead, she leaned over to give him an encore kiss.

"Laura," he said, "be safe. And see you Sunday. If you need anything or if you change your mind, call me. You've got my number."

"You know I'm not changing my mind." Besides, she thought, if anything goes wrong, I can remove the amulet.

It did rain that night and hard. Laura didn't make it out as far into the forest as she had hoped to. It's okay, she told herself, though she was feeling like less of a Cheryl Strayed type badass than she had been when the trip began.

But it wasn't like she was hiking the Pacific Rim Trail. She was just attempting a three-day hike of moderate difficulty in a run-of-the-mill state park.

    The first day had been long and hard and grueling. She hadn't put on enough sunscreen or big spray and her hiking socks were too thick for her shoes. Rather than feeling rejuvenated like she had hoped, she felt soaked and itchy and sore. She wanted to cuddle up inside her tent and sleeping bag, but she hadn't yet pitched her tent. Maybe, she thought, I could just sleep on the wet ground like the ancient people. (Wait, did the ancient people even do that? She really wasn't sure. Or did they just live in caves? Like why would they allow themselves to be pelted with rain when they had other options?) Laura was tempted to call Jack. She knew that he would be there in a jiffy if she just called and asked. Instead, she counted to ten and began the wet work of setting up her camp. Only after that could she finally curl up inside her warm tent and listen to the rain failing in the forest as she drifted into a hard-earned sleep.

    The next morning, loud birds woke her. They had birds in the city, of course, but amid all the other noises—the honking of horns, the hailing of taxis, and the roaring of buses—it was harder to hear them. Here, everything felt so peaceful and pure. Laura got out a can of coffee and one of her MREs and gnawed at the prepackaged underspiced foods hungrily. She didn't even care that the meat was cold and her blonde hair was frizzy from this morning's humidity and last night's rain. She ate with purpose, quick but not too quick. She wanted to leave early enough so that she could make up the time she had lost. The weather you couldn't control, but your response to the weather you could. Out in the wilderness, Laura thought of her mother as she walked because she associated her mother with wilderness. The second day, she doubled her time and her distance. She hiked till dark.

Laura didn't talk about what happened to her mother. Usually, she even didn't even think about it. But, tonight, her memory took her back to her twelfth birthday when her mother had fastened the amulet around her neck. "Daughter," she said, "this amulet will give you control. But there might be a time when you need to lose control. However, do not do this lightly. For, if you lose control, you might not ever be able to get it back. And there may be a time when I might need to go to the forest, and I might not come back," her mother said, her dark eyes looking into Laura's blue ones. Laura had nodded, as if she understood. But she hadn't, and maybe she never would. She and her mother were so different. Everything about her mother seemed to be a contrast to Laura herself. Dark eyes, dark hair compared to Laura's light ones. Her mother loved the countryside. Laura lived in the busy bustling city. It was only a 45-minute drive, but it felt farther, longer. It felt like she and her mother had lived in different worlds. As the sun began to set, the temperature dropped to a comfortable 65 degrees. She heard the buzzing of crickets and watched the glowing of fireflies and remembered how much she loved the darkness, the quiet of the woods.

But then Laura heard dissonant noises. Men laughing coarsely, loudly, past the point of civility, Laura decided to make herself quiet, remain in the leaves. But one of the men, drunk, stumbling, wandered over to where Laura was, in fact he ran right into her.

"Hey, little lady," he said with past-his-prime frat boy charm. "Why don't you come join me and my friends by the fire?"

"No, thanks, I'm good," Laura said.

The man called for his country bumpkin friends. "Leroy! Larry! Look what I founded out here in the forest!" LeRoy was tall. Larry and the man who had called for him were squat and fat. Likely brothers, Laura thought.

"I don't want any trouble," Laura said, feeling as she said it that she was a walking cliche. Woman outnumbered. Women in peril. Woman alone in the forest. She didn't want to be any kind of warning to other women.

"My boyfriend, he just went back down to the car to get some gear," Laura lied. But it was a bad lie.

Even drunk, the men knew this was bullshit. The trailhead was at least 10 miles away. Shit, Laura thought. Again, Laura hoped that the men would leave or let her leave, so she wouldn't have to take her mother's advice.

"Come on, baby girl," the first brother, whose name she didn't know, said. The men surrounded her, thinking they could overpower her. She could see why they would think this, but they misunderstood who and what she was.

Laura gave them one last warning. "Back up," she said. "Or I might have to kill you."

The men laughed. "What are you, a Kung Fu master or something?" And they did their best racist impression of martial arts. They began to approach her from all sides. And then Laura ripped the amulet off.

What came next her mother hadn't warned her about. Metamorphosis. Lost time. Confusion. Waking up in a place and not knowing how she got there. In this case, a steep slope that she had to climb down. Naked. That was the best/worst part. At least if she had still been a wolf, she could blend in with the setting more easily. And people would run from her, making it easier to cross long distances quickly.

"Transformation," her mother had told her, "is never easy." At the time, Laura had wanted to laugh. It seemed like such an obvious thing to say. What other great life advice had her mother given her? "A stitch in time saves nine." Laura thought. "A penny saved is a penny earned." But these, she knew, weren't really things her mother had told her. They were just generic sayings.

Last night, Laura could have killed those men, but she hadn't. She wondered if her mother would have killed them. Instead of killing them, she had only hurt them enough to scare them, stop them, make them think twice the next time they thought they could overpower a woman. Laura couldn't ask her mother what she would have done because her mother had left for the forest and never returned. Couldn't her mother have left her something practical, tangible, step-by-step, like *A Girl's Guide to Werewolfing and Wood Prowling*, or *Wolf Words of Wisdom*. Like anything other than leaving with no explanation.

Now, that she was back to human, Laura didn't have her warm fur, and she missed it. She wasn't naked and afraid, just naked and cold. Naked and annoyed. Naked and . . . Laura realized that she did still have some of her other powers.

"Men," her mother had told her, "each have a unique scent. When you love one, you never forget his smell." Rob had smelled like car grease and Marie's perfume. That should have been a sign, would have been a sign, if Laura had been smart enough to listen to her instincts. Instead, she listened to the friends who told her that Rob was great, such a catch. A businessman, an entrepreneur. He was rich, and, if he was rich, he must be smart. If he was successful, he must be kind. He had all of the bad qualities of powerful men, and none of the good ones. Except he was rich, he was charming, he was physically attractive.

Jack, on the other hand, was both less and more attractive. He was shorter, fatter, poorer, but he . . . Laura thought of the smell of him. It was pine and leather and Fritos and bacon. Maybe bacon Fritos. Jack liked his junk food and his red meat. Maybe if I can, Laura thought. Laura tracked the smell of vehicles to the road and then after that she searched for the smell of Jack. Would it be enough, she wondered, to help her get back to him, back to the city, back home.

Though she didn't have her fur or her clothes or her phone, Laura had two other things—super smell and super speed. She could run back to the city quickly. Had she run like this yesterday, she could have run the length of the park, could have escaped the men. But she couldn't do any of these things with the amulet on. With the amulet off, however . . .

Laura closed her eyes and sniffed for it. Bacon, Fritos, pine. She made a few wrong turns, but then, running on all fours, she reached the city, the smell of Jack growing stronger. The smell of his neighborhood, his block, his apartment. She jumped to his balcony and gently knocked on the window. Jack was hung over and asleep. She could tell that through the window. So she knocked harder, thinking if he doesn't come over here and open this window, I'm going to have to break it. But then Jack finally did wake up and stumble over to the window.

"Laura?" he asked. "What are you doing here? How did you get up here, and where are your clothes?"

"Open the window," she said, "and I'll explain."

He looked down. "There's no ladder to the ground,"

he said, "and I'm four stories up. Are you Catwoman or something?"

"The window, please," she said. And he opened it and let her in. "You're close," she said, "but wrong family. You're thinking cats. Think dogs. Don't you want to know how I got all the way back here?"

"To be honest, I'm more wondering about what happened to your clothes."

"I followed your scent," she said. "Bacon, Fritos, and pine. My mother was a werewolf, and she said that you never forget the smell of the men you love. Rob was—"

"You love me?" Jack said with confusion. He was shirtless, and Laura could see clearly how fat he had gotten in the last year, but Laura was naked, and she was hungry.

"Did you miss the part of that story where I told you that my mother was a werewolf?"

"No, it's just more believable to me than the other thing. I mean look at me," he said gesturing to his protruding gut, "and look at you." And he was looking at her.

"I'm hungry," she repeated, her meaning unmistakable. "And I ran all the way back from the forest."

"While I appreciate your enthusiasm, why didn't you just call?" Jack asked.

Laura sighed. The men, the forest. "Usually, I wore an amulet. To tame the wolf, but I took it off, and without it, the wolf might be harder to control. But I am the wolf, and the wolf is me. But I had to take it off because of these redneck men, who wanted to—"

"Wait, some crazy men tried to attack you, and you didn't call?"

"Are you even listening? I had to change into a werewolf to fend them off. I could have killed them, but I didn't. It took great control not to kill them, but I didn't. Now, it's taking great control, not to," she began. She closed her eyes and sniffed him.

"You can let go," he said.

"But you have to understand," she said.

"I understand." He kissed her.

And then she closed her eyes and unleashed the wolf.

"Wow," Jack said, "that was a first."

"A good first or a bad first?"

"It was a little distracting," he admitted, "when you started growling."

"But," she said, "it was a happy growl."

"I feel like a happy purr might be easier to handle."

"But my mother wasn't a tiger. She was a werewolf."

"Did Rob know?"

"No," she said, "I kept the amulet on, and it never came up."

"So, he never got to experience whatever that was in bed?"

"No," she said.

"He was an idiot to leave you."

"Because I'm a werewolf?"

"Because you're beautiful and kind. And he was neither of those things."

"He was handsome," she acknowledged.

"Only on the outside," he said. "On the inside, he was rotten as a corpse and maybe just as soulless. You deserve better. But I'm not sure I'm better. I have issues."

"I know, Jack. You eat too much, and you drink too much, and you hate yourself for it, but you do it anyway. And you think that's why you're alone. You don't want to be alone. But you think that you're too much of a disaster for anyone to love you, but I know you, and I love you. I mean, we all have issues."

"What are your issues?"

"I'm a werewolf," she said. "Like literally a werewolf. I mean wouldn't you say that's kind of an issue?"

"I think we could make it work though," he said.

"Yeah?" she said hopefully. "Will you try to tame me?"

"Only if you want me to, but I have to admit," he said. "I like you either way. Also, if you need some clothes that won't fit you right, let me know. But, you know, if you just want to walk around naked, I'm completely okay with that too."

He smiled. She loved his smile. In fact, she thought it might be the most beautiful smile she had ever seen because he knew who and what she was, and, even knowing all that, he had no plans to leave.

"Next time, you'll come with me," she said.

He groaned.

"I'm a werewolf, so you can't not ask me to go into the forest. And, if you're worried about my safety, come. Protect me."

"I don't think you need me to protect me," he said.

"I don't, but I also don't want to be alone in the forest."

"You're not," he said. "You're not alone. There, here, or anywhere."

The Girl in the Mirror

I didn't talk to the girl in the mirror, at least not at first. Even though we looked alike, we were not the same. I didn't know where her world was, but what I did know was that her world wasn't mine.

The similarities were this. We both had short black hair, pale skin, and glasses like Peppermint Patty's friend Marcie. But Mirror Girl wore pink barrettes in her hair and sometimes crimped it.

Normally, I just curled mine under to straighten, it if I did anything at all.

Mirror Girl's life seemed more glamorous than mine. She groomed herself for parties and dances.

I checked and rechecked my crappy credit score at Lending Tree, read spam emails from Jane Fonda about climate change, and tried to pretend like Jennifer Aniston's *Friends* character was my bff. Mirror Girl's life seemed so extra compared to mine, so, when she reached her hand through the mirror, I took it.

When I got through to the other side, I expected lights, drinks, and music. Instead, it was cold and dark and nothing like the glimpses I had seen. I stood in a forest encircled by trees. The trees tried to grab and hold me. I looked through the mirror at my old crappy life with longing. I could see my messy apartment. It now seemed like a castle compared to this prison. The mirror was still there, but the portal had closed. There was no way out.

The Vampire Accountant

You wake up one morning and you feel different, better. You haven't felt this alive in well—really never. It's like you were dead, but you were never dead. At least you don't think you were dead. You really don't remember all the details.

Missy's father was the one who died. And you flew down South, down home to attend the funeral. You never take personal days, so your boss was like, "Sure, Leslie, go, go." And then you were there on a plane, sipping your Coke in the plastic cup. And then you were there, graveside, watching them lower that man your father's age into the sweaty summer ground.

And then you said to Missy, "Hey, honey. I'm so sorry." Put your hand on her shoulder. And she said, "Lakeside," and you were so relieved. *That* you could do, even though you hadn't done it in years. You could go to the lake and smoke pot. You knew that ritual, even though you hadn't done the thing, not like that, not with Missy and the boys you used to hang out with. She used to hang out with badass motorcycle boys, who overlooked you because you were the brainy one. Pale-faced, straitlaced. You didn't let your boobs hang out, and Missy, well, she was bawdy, messy. Big butt, big boobs, a girl the boys were all over. And then she had Tyler and Taylor and Tommy. And you went to school and more school and got that good job at the accounting firm in Chicago.

"I'll be back," you told your parents, who drank sweet tea and nodded sadly on the porch. You did come home sometimes. Though not as often as they wanted you to and more often than you wanted to.

Your mom said, yesterday, or maybe the day before, "Any plans for marriage?" There had been men, but the men wanted sex, sex, and more sex. And you didn't mind sex, but, after a while, sex with no ring got tiresome. And then they cheated. You never cheated. Or they said they'd call and didn't. And you realized you were expendable.

Middle-class, middle of the road, a take-home-for-dinner-with-your-parents kind of girl but not the one they really wanted underneath the sheets.

"Oh, I met Layla," they said. "And Kayla. And Shayla." And girls with more exciting, unmistakably female names.

But the thing that happened, it was after the pot. And after Missy's boyfriend tried to hit on you. She had three kids and wasn't looking as good as she used to. And you said "no, no, no," and then maybe you said yes. She used to make fun of you. Remember that: "Lesbo Leslie." *Eff you, Missy. Eff you.* But you never said that. You just sat there tight lipped and took it.

So what if you did make out with Karl? And then Christian. Or was his name darker? Like Draco Malfoy or something from *Harry Potter*.

So what if there was maybe something with a bat? And then a bite the size of a big embarrassing hickey. And then your eyes, your face. Pale white skin and red eyes that kind of glow. But, for some reason, no one's noticing the eyes, or if they are, they aren't saying.

Your mother says you look good, despite the bat bite. You worry about rabies. Call a doctor. Seduce the doctor. He's married. You're not that kind of girl, yet you don't care. You suck his blood or something like that. Maybe no blood. But lots of biting. At least some biting. And maybe blood but not that kind of bleeding.

And then you go home. Wear dark glasses during the day.

Your boss says, "Ah, Leslie. What happened? Your skin's so pale." And he looks at you in a way that he has never looked at you. Approvingly. And you wear red bras and white shirts that aren't buttoned up far enough, and no one says, "Oh you shouldn't do that. Shouldn't wear that." Shouldn't be that kind of girl. The kind of girl you always hated, feared. Now, you are her.

And then you meet a guy on the El. He's wearing a nice white shirt and sporting slicked back James Dean hair. And you like him, like him a lot. He likes Gothic novels. Especially Mary Shelley and Bram Stoker. He tells you this, why, you don't know, but you go with it. You're chill now.

"You like *Dracula*?" you say.

He says, "Yeah, it's great."

"You like *Twilight*?" you say.

He says, "No, it's shit."

You laugh. You haven't read *Dracula* or *Twilight*. They were on your list of things to million things to read that you never got to. You were too busy crunching numbers, but now you think you might make time.

He says he's getting off next stop, Lake Street.

You say you're staying on a while, going all the way to Cermak/Chinatown. You don't know why you say this. You never go there. Truth is, some of the streets around there are kinda sketchy. But you are no longer afraid.

"Wanna come?" you ask.

He says no. Then he looks at you in your white shirt, red bra, reconsiders.

And then you go to the South Side to neighborhoods you would have never dreamed of going to before and you walk through them like you own them, like a modern day

She-Ra, Princess of Power.

"You like me?" you ask.

It's like some old-time bodice ripping romance novel cover. It's fucking windy and your shirt is half off.

He smiles. He's just looking at your boobs. But it's not like that, you tell yourself.

"Wanna go see the White Sox play?" you say, even though you couldn't care less about baseball.

He nods, says yes. He buys you popcorn, peanuts. His hand is on your leg.

Sometime later, you're back on the El. Sometime later, you're on the Purple Line. Going out of the city headed north.

He says, as you head into Evanston, "People don't dress like that here."

He hands you his jacket.

"Where are we going?" you ask.

He names some swanky high rise.

"For sex?" you ask.

Now that you're a vampire, what is there but sex and blood? Was there ever more than that? Was there ever less?

"What do you think?" he says. And he doesn't seem so sexy anymore. His slicked back hair just looks greasy now. He is greasy and sleazy.

"I see, I guess,"you say. But, even now, in your slutty, skanky clothes, you want more.

"I think I'm going back to Howard," you say, but he turns mean.

He says, "I don't think so."

This whole El scene could turn ugly. But then like some Avenger Thor-looking-dude comes out of nowhere to help.

You throw that MoFo from the train. But just onto a

platform. No one really says anything or does anything. This is Chicago. People are used to minding their own business and ignoring the man selling *StreetWise*, playing saxophone on the street corner, or prophesying the end of days.

Now, you turn your attention to Avenger dude. You think you've seen him before on the El. In attorney-looking day clothes. But now he's in his fight for justice save the damsel in distress night clothes. And he's really fine. Avenger dude sits with you. He knows your name.

"Hey, Leslie. You alright?"

"He just—. They all just—. Want sex," you say.

"Isn't that why you became a vampire?" he says. He's all black sunglasses and long coat, circa 1999. So much better than the attorney suits, you think.

"Dude, are you like Morpheus?"

He laughs. "Wanna pill?" He reaches into his pocket like he has one.

"No," you say. Or maybe yes. "But my old life, that kinda sucked too."

He asks if you wanna go to some hippy thrift shop in Belmont. You say no, then yes. He says coffee. You say no, then yes. And then there's sex and more sex. And blood. And rock n' roll.

"What now?" you ask.

He seems darker, but the darkness is comforting rather than alarming, and you want to embrace it, embrace him, unlock all its messy, sweaty, scary secrets.

When he says, "Are you sure you're ready," you don't hesitate. Now you own the darkness.

Hot Dog from Heaven

There was much debate about what to call the flying object in the sky.

"It's a bird, it's a plane, it's . . . ." Dad was a Superman fanatic, so, of course, he would try to relate it to the Man of Steel.

"It's a UFO," Mary said decisively. She was the oldest, the tallest, and she was used to being right. Also, she was going through a *Beetlejuice* faze, so, of course, she would try to come up with some alarming explanation.

I looked at the sky carefully. It wasn't a UFO though because it wasn't unidentified. "It's a hot dog," I said.

Mom, who was trying to pretend like she didn't need glasses, squinted at the object. "Julie's right," she said. "It's a hot dog. Now can we go back to eating our dinner?" Mom took a big bite out of the corn on the cob on her plastic picnic plate, as if she was ready to move on. The rest of us just kept staring up.

"But why," Claire asked, "is a giant hot dog flying through the sky?"

"She does make a good point," Mary noted.

I, too, kept looking at the giant weenie. For once, the three of us were in agreement: This was weird. And Dad was probably still trying to think of a way to relate the hot dog back to Superman.

We weren't the only ones to notice the flying hot dog. The other families at the park were also looking up. There were lots of families out there since the weather was nice for late summer/early fall, and people wanted to enjoy the moderate temperatures while they could.

Mary began look concerned, as if she wanted to say something.

"Okay, what?" I finally asked.

"That thing seems to be moving awfully fast," Mary said with concern.

"And?" I said knowing that Doomsday Mary wanted to say more. I fiddled with my baked beans. I was never a fan of syrup-covered beans or farting, and I wondered if, while everyone was looking up, I could sneak my beans into the closest public trashcan.

"Speed," continued Mary, "is distance over time, and force equals mass times acceleration."

I grew impatient. "So what are you trying to say, Einstein?"

"Actually, I was thinking of Newton's Second Law of Motion," Mary explained, as if I knew what she was talking about or cared. I seriously considered squirting the bottle of mustard on her. Exasperated, Mary finally said, "An object that big going that fast is going to cause some serious damage."

"Why didn't you just say that in the first place?" I asked. She looked at me as if I was a moron, so I said, "You know it's really too hot to be wearing so much black in summer."

"OMG, Julie, focus. We have to prevent that object from hitting the earth at the speed it's going, or—"

"How?" I asked, as I tried to see if Mom still had her eyes on the trash can. She was digging into a second piece of corn and watching that thing like a hawk.

"Could we squirt it with mustard," Claire asked, "to slow it down?"

"If only we could shoot laser beams from our eyes," Dad muttered.

"Give it a rest, Frank." Mom said.

"According to Newton's First Law of Physics," Mary began. We all gave her a look. "Okay, fine, we can slow it down by speeding it up in the other direction."

"So we could shoot at it?" Dad said.

"Yes, but," Mary said.

"With what?" I asked.

"Anything we have," Claire said.

Dad ran to the Jeep to go get his pistol. Claire grabbed her water guns.

Mom told the other families in language plain enough for them to understand, "We need to shoot that giant weenie to stop it from hitting us."

They agreed that no one wanted a weenie shiner.

Other families grabbed what they could: barbeque sauce, Nerf rockets, BB guns, slingshots, tennis ball blasters, paint balls. Some guy with a *Don't Tread on Me* license plate even pulled out a Remington R15.

Mary got out a piece of paper and started writing down calculations, which, in my opinion, wasn't particularly helpful at the moment. But I just let Mary be Mary. Besides, she had a terrible throwing arm. I gathered up all the balls I could find: Soccer, football, baseball, even a dodge ball or two. Claire helped me fling them. Mom threw some chicken bones, and inspired by her use of food for ammo, I threw the rest of the baked beans, including the ones still on my plate. Mom looked horrified because she had made those nasty things from scratch.

"What?" I shrugged. "I'm just doing my part to save the planet."

"Just don't throw the pudding dessert," Dad said, and Claire nodded agreement. We kept on shooting at the hot dog, everything we could, and, finally, the thing began to break into apart, and small bite-sized weenie pieces began to rain down from the sky. The ones that hit us felt like hail, and somehow Mary, lost in calculations, ended up with a golf ball sized weenie knot on her head.

Thankfully, there wasn't as much damage as there could have been because, once the hot dog bits started falling, hounds showed up from all directions to snap up the delicious treats. Then they rolled around happily in the grass.

Once most of the weenie debris had settled, Mom unwrapped the pudding dessert, and we all dug in. The pudding and the cream cheese was wonderful, but shooing the dogs away was a little annoying.

"This is heavenly," Claire said.

Mary just rubbed her head while I ate without talking.

"I'd say," added Dad, "that it's out of this world."

"For once," Mom said, "we'll allow it."

We all nodded as we devoured the pudding dessert and watched the dogs begin to scatter back to wherever they had come from.

Outside Eden

They told us not to enter the green room, and, at first, we didn't. We didn't even want to. Why would we, when we could bask in the bright sunlight of the yellow room, the earthy shade of the brown room, the love vibes coming from the pink room, or the winning energy that emanated from the prized silver and gold room?

Among athletes and children, the silver and gold room was the favorite. It was frequented by prize fighters, kindergartners learning to count money, and rock stars who liked their bling. It reminded people of Christmas, tinfoil-wrapped chocolate, and victory.

The pink room was the room of choice for preadolescent girls who thought that they were in love with the latest teen heartthrob and of grandmothers who wanted to remember their wild and lusty youths. It was pink hearts, pink flowers, bubble baths, cotton candy, and sleek pink joy.

Yellow was the chosen color of both those prone to depression and the naturally happy. People associated it with lemonade, movie theater butter popcorn, and sunflowers. It made them feel light and airy, warm, bright, loved.

The brown room was preferred by gardeners, landscapers, construction workers, and macho, macho men. It made people think of leaves, s'mores, yule logs, and chocolate. Every other Wednesday, the brown room was filled with the aromas of hot cocoas, gourmet lattes, and Teddy Grahams. That was when the Better Off in the Brown Room Club met. The smells of all things brown roasted, brown baked, and braised in brown were tempting, but I was a team yellow loyalist.

"Hey," Chris shouted at me as I attempted to sneak by with a box of Lemonheads in my hand and return to my little world of brightness, "Why don't you join us, Mel?"

"No, I can't," I said. I was thinking of lilies and Lay's chips.

"We have the best beer here," Joel added. I had never liked beer, so that didn't tempt me.

Lemon meringue pie, on the other hand. Lemon loaf. Lemon bars. With all things light and beautiful firmly in my head, I scurried off, intending to head straight to the glow of the yellow lava lamp just inside.

But something, or rather someone, stopped me. It was Bobby, whose favorite color was black, and who lurked in the hallway like a menacing shadow. The brown room wasn't dark enough for him, and he couldn't stand the sight of anything warm or comforting. "Hey," I said, my mind firmly on lemon cake. "How's it going?"

"Why do you think we can't go in the green room?" he asked.

I stopped. Now he had my attention. We didn't talk about the green room. Normally, we didn't want to. I believed what they said. They kept us away for our own good. They kept us away to protect us.

"Green is the color of anger, of jealousy, of aliens, and Mr. Yuck stickers," I said, mindlessly repeating what they had told us.

"But isn't it also the color of limes, leaves, and Leprechauns?" Bobby asked, his red brown hair forming a cartoon character cowlick.

"Leprechauns," I said skeptically. "You believe in leprechauns?"

He shrugged. "What can I say? I'm Irish. I mean isn't

every color good or bad, depending on what you do with it? And how is doing what they say all the time any better than the blind loyalty that our ancestors had to nations?"

All of this was a little heavy, I thought, for a Friday night.

"Um, look, it's late," I said. "I need to go." Bobby seemed to realize that he was behaving frantically and backed off.

"Sure, yeah, sorry," he said.

But when I got inside the yellow room, I didn't feel the usual warmth bouncing off and through me like sunbeams. Instead, I felt sour and confused, like a used lemon rind or the seedy bottom of a lemonade, and I didn't even want to take a candy from the seemingly endless bowl of lemon Starbursts.

Clarissa, a perky blond who was wearing a pineapple costume and roller skates, offered me a fresh slice of lemon loaf. Even though the cake was still steaming and dripping in warm glaze, and usually I loved lemon loaf, I declined. What if Bobby was right, I wondered. What if there was more out there in the green room like mint chip ice cream and shamrock cookies, and the board wanted to keep it from us?

Usually, I didn't pay attention to the reading materials about the history of color schemes and happiness. But I kept them in a folder in the plastic shelving unit beneath my bed just in case I ever needed them. In the time before, we learned history. But now we just, what was it that we were doing with our lives? I tossed and turned all night. Normally, the yellow stars I had carefully placed on the ceiling were a comfort to me. But now they and everything else in the yellow room seemed like overkill. Why did we have to pick one color and stay true to it? Why weren't we allowed to explore them all? And why did we only focus on four colors? Why were there no oranges, reds, or blues?

The signage outside the green room seemed like overkill. *Caution. Danger. Keep Out.* Bobby and I navigated our way through it until we pushed our way to the door. The door was locked. Right outside the door was another ominous sign. *If you've made it this far, turn back before it's too late.* Too late for what, I wondered. To make better style choices? Why were some colors revered and others hated? Why did we have to rank and categorize everything into groups of good, better, best? Bobby had pilfered a key from a guard who was blacked out from drinking too much beer in the brown room last night, but, of course, the key didn't work. We had come so far and through what seemed like an obstacle course of difficulties, that it seemed like a waste to give up now. There was the door right in front of us. All we had to do was find a way to get through it. It was then that we saw the fingerprint scanners.

"Hey," I said to Bobby, "why don't we give those a try?"

A sign flashed that said, "Dual control is required."

"I guess that means we're supposed to scan both our fingerprints at the same time?" I said to Bobby, who seemed on edge.

"Look, Mel, maybe we should just . . ." But we had come too far to go back to where we'd been.

"Bobby, put your finger on the scanner." 3, 2, 1.

"DNA match detected. Welcome, daughter of the founder and trusted friend."

Bobby gave me a look. "Daughter of the founder?"

"Trusted friend, I have no idea. I don't know anything more about this than you do. But now that the door is open, don't you want to go in and check it out?"

He shrugged. "I guess." After hesitating a moment, we pushed open the door. Inside, the walls were green, the carpet was green, the furniture was green. But it didn't beckon those who entered to want to stay. It was as if green was just a color, nothing more, nothing less. There was no food in the green room and no people.

"That was kind of anticlimactic," I said, and Bobby agreed. We didn't know what so scary about this room. It seemed benign, boring, harmless. We didn't know what else to do, so we left. But I didn't want to go back to the yellow room, and he didn't want to continue sulking in the hallway. So we made a plan to return to the green room the next day and maybe paint it. "We could add vines," I said. "And maybe frogs."

In the meantime, I wanted to do some research on this place and on who my father, the founder, had been. We all hung out here in the rooms of our choice, but we never talked about who our parents had been or how we had gotten here. It seemed strange to me that the machine that ran the fingerprint scanner knew more about me than I did.

I had grabbed some books on the history of the color colony and brought them with me on our next trip to the green room. We had so many plans about how we wanted to decorate it, but when we got there, oddly enough, all we wanted to do was sleep. Instead of painting or reading, we cuddled under green blankets, which had appeared out of nowhere, it seemed, and slept for what, an hour, two hours, three? I wasn't really sure. When we woke up though, we still felt tired. I yawned. He yawned. And we both fell back to sleep. When we woke up again, we were surprised to find ourselves naked under the covers. Seriously, where were our clothes? What happened next wasn't much of a surprise because we weren't dead, and bodies against bodies usually make you feel things. When we woke up, we had our clothes back and wondered if all of that had been a dream. But, if it had been a dream, at least it had a nice one.

"Um, maybe we should go back," he said.

"Yeah," I agreed. We were both a little stunned. Once we moved back into the main corridor, we went our separate ways. But, that night, I dreamed of Bobby and me. We were naked and bathed in green, and the dreams were so pleasant that I didn't want to wake up. In fact, I didn't wake up until almost noon, which, for me, was late. I thought that I should maybe read about my father, the founder, but that thought was fleeting. More interesting and urgent was the need to find Bobby. When I left the yellow room, I saw him standing outside in the corridor, as if he was waiting. "So we're going, right?" he said.

I nodded even though we had not discussed this possibility the day before. When we got closer to the green room, there weren't forbidding signs this time but instead green arrows. "Green means go," I thought, and we rushed into the green room as quickly as we could. There was a green banner this time. It said welcome Founder's Daughter and Partner. That was a step up from trusted friend, I thought. Behind the sign was a green bed. The room clearly wanted us to get on it, and who were we to argue? This time we didn't need to be lulled to sleep and have our clothes removed in order to participate. We were ready and willing to engage on our own. I still wondered if yesterday was a dream, but Bobby answered my question by saying, "Wow, that was even better than before." Afterward, I asked if we should go. "Nah," Bobby said, "let's see what happens if we stay." After an hour or two, we were starting to get hungry, and the room, as if anticipating our needs, provided us with spinach, avocados, green beans, mint rubbed lamb, key lime pie, and creme de menthe parfaits. All that food made us sleepy, but, before we slept, we kissed, and went at it again.

The next morning, when we woke up, we were still in the green room. Without discussion, we removed our clothes and found each other again.

"This is my favorite room," I said dreamily.

"But, Mel, do you think it's a trap?"

"I don't care. Do you care?"

"No," he admitted.

"What should we do now?" I asked.

Just then, a pool of green appeared. "Oh, my gosh, just look at all those green apples." And trees. Suddenly we were surrounded.

"I think maybe we shouldn't eat the apples," I said to him. "I think maybe something bad happens if we do?"

"What about the green grapes?" he asked.

"I think maybe we could make a vine," I suggested. And the weather in here is so nice that I don't think we need to put our clothes back on. I mean unless you want to."

He shook his head. We got naked in the green pool and drank green drinks and laughed and splashed and played. When it seemed like the appropriate time, we got back into the green bed and fell blissfully asleep.

After a time, we wondered if we should go back and check on the others. Did anyone miss us or even notice that we were gone?

"Maybe we should check on them?" I suggested.

"Yeah," he agreed. But neither of us really wanted to go. Still, we felt like we needed to. We asked the room for clothes, and, at first, it tried to give us green leaves to wear. But I shouted back, "Okay, we love these leaves. These leaves are super cool, but we can't really wear them outside this room, so could we have our actual old boring clothes back? We promise that we'll take them off when we come back."

The room seemed to hem and haw before it finally acquiesced and dumped our clothes from the sky. As we left the green room, the air began to feel heavier and so did I, as if my body... I turned to Bobby. "Do I look okay?"

"You look fabulous," he said.

But I felt like he wasn't really seeing me for how I was.

"I feel like it's hard to breathe out here," I said.

"Mel, we'll meet back in half an hour outside the yellow room," he said.

I nodded. Bobby was headed toward the brown room, I think. It was the room he felt the most kinship with, even though he didn't really have a color home outside of the green room. Was the green room our home now? I wondered as I trudged slowly through the thick air. Inside the yellow room, I saw Clarissa with a tray of lemon loaf. She didn't even offer me one, which I thought was rude.

"Oh, hey, Mel. You were gone so long that we thought you were dead. But you just got fat."

Stunned, I wasn't sure how to reply. "Um, yeah," I said. "Just out of curiosity," I said, "how long has it been since you've last seen me?"

"Like six months. Look, I don't want to tell you what to do, but this is what happens when you spend too much time in the brown room. And we've been talking."

"Who is *we*?" I asked.

"You know, us yellow girls." I started at her white-yellow hair and couldn't help thinking that she looked like one of the children of the corn. With a creepy grin, she added, "And none of us think that dark boy is right for you. Sometimes, it's better for yellow people and dark people not to mix." I breathed deeply, but the heavy air made me feel like I was choking.

"Okay, well thanks for that," I said because I didn't know what else to say. I wanted to leave, but first I had to pee. I squeezed into the nearest yellow room. The lemon scent was suffocating. After I peed, I looked at myself in the mirror. I didn't look fat, I looked. . .

"Oh my God," I thought. I gathered up a few things: a picture of my parents, a beaded necklace I had made as a child, some hair clips. There is surprisingly little that I wanted or needed from this place. I went to find Bobby outside the yellow room, but he wasn't there. Panicking, I started to walk the hallway. I found him outside the brown room laughing and talking to some friends. One of them asked him, "Did you knock that yellow girl up?"

Bobby looked from them to me and them to me again. I felt lightheaded and sweaty. Regardless of what Bobby decided to do, I knew I needed to get back to the green room. So I started walking. Bobby caught up to me a minute or two later. I was breathing heavily and walking slowly, so it wasn't hard.

"Hey, Mel," he said, "I got you."

"Yeah?" I asked.

"Yeah," he said, and he took my hand. Together, we walked to the green room.

When we got there, the doors opened for us automatically saying, "Welcome, mother and father of the future."

"This omniscient door is really getting on my nerves," I said. But we went in anyway. Once inside, the air felt cleaner, purer. There was a large video screen with the words *welcome home* on it. In front of the screen were two movie theater style seats with drink holders. Bobby got coffee, and I got water. When we sat down, it seemed to activate the video. There were two people on the screen who looked vaguely like ancient Greeks, but I knew from the picture that I had carried back with me that they were my parents, but with whiter hair. On the video screen, they kind of looked like Jor-El and Lara though from *Superman*. The first thing I said, before I could think better of it was, "So am I an alien?"

"Greetings, Melanie," my mother said, not even bothering to dignify my question with a response. Bobby gave me a wtf look, so I sighed and said, "Oh, hey, Mom, Dad."

"Our time here is limited," Dad said, "so we need you to listen carefully."

"Because you're dead?" I asked.

"Our bodies have entered the astral plane," he said.

"That kind of seems like it means they're dead," I said to Bobby, who nodded.

"You know we can hear you," my father said with annoyance.

"Okay, sorry. What's this big important message?"

"Have you read the colony's pamphlets?" my mother asked in what sounded to me like teacher voice.

"So, about that, funny story," I began.

My father interrupted, "If you haven't read them, don't bother," he said. "They're pure propaganda."

"Okay, cool," I said, pleased that my procrastination

and lack of motivation had paid off for once.

"What you need to know," my father continued, as if I hadn't interrupted him, "is that the way things are isn't the way we intended them to be."

"This was supposed to be utopia," my mother added mournfully.

I rolled my eyes.

"What?" my mother asked.

"Well, it's just that, are you all not familiar with stories about utopias? *The Giver*? *Logan's Run*? Do they *ever* work out well?"

"Did you read those?" my mother asked hopefully.

No, I admitted. I had seen the movies, but that was not the point.

"Oh," my mother said with disappointment.

My father seemed to be getting annoyed with both of us. "The point is," he continued, "that we wanted to create to space that honored all the colors. We didn't intend to create a space that separated people by color. But, after the first few years, things went terribly wrong."

"Well, if that's the case, then why is this room all green?"

"I'm glad that you asked," my father said, sounding pleased. "It is, but it isn't. You see this room isn't just a room. It's a gateway."

"To what?" I asked.

"To a world with all the colors," my father said. "And all you have to do to get there is climb the beanstalk."

"Seriously," I said.

"What?" my mother asked.

"I'm like six months pregnant, and you're asking me climb a beanstalk?"

"To be fair," my mother said smugly, "we didn't

expect you to get pregnant this quickly, but given . . . "

My cheeks flushed deep red. "You took our clothes and provided us first with only blankets and then only a bed. What did you expect us to do?"

To my surprise, my father came to my defense. "She does have a point, Rebecca. Remember when we were her age, and we. . ."

"Oh, Isaac," my mother laughed.

"Seriously," I said, "can you please just not?"

"It's true that this is an unanticipated obstacle," my father said. "But we could help you with this. We could provide elves to help you up the beanstalk."

I was speechless, but Bobby stepped up. "No, we're good. If Melanie needs help, I can help her."

"See, Rebecca, I told you. He is a gentleman," my father said.

"It's just that I expected her to choose someone a little less handsome. I mean, look at her. She has put on a lot of weight."

I stared at them, open mouthed. Bobby turned to me, whispered, "Hey, baby, you look beautiful."

I smiled. When I looked back over at my mother and father, they were both staring at us.

"See," my father said, "he's very sweet."

Bobby took my hand. To them, he said, "Your daughter is the most beautiful woman I have ever seen. And I'm not going anywhere."

"Well," my father said, "you two probably have things to do, so we'll let you go."

"Wait," I said urgently, "I have questions. Like can we eat the apples?"

"Yes," my father said. "The apples are fine. Why wouldn't they be?"

"It's just, you know, that whole forbidden fruit thing."

"Melanie, nothing is forbidden," my father said. "If that's all, then . . ."

"No," I said, almost desperately, "that's not all. If we're supposed to be fruitful and multiply, and there's only the two of us here, then how?"

"Don't worry about that," my father said. "When the time is right, their partners will find their way here, just like you did. Anything else?"

"Are there leprechauns? Or could there be?" Bobby asked.

My mother and I both gave him a look.

"Okay, well, we should be going," my mother said. "But we'll be in touch."

"But I don't know how to," I began.

"I'll send instructions on childbirth and parenting," my mother said. "And I'll make sure it's a video, so you won't have to read anything, Melanie."

And just like that, they were gone, though the huge video screen remained. We looked around. On the wall near the door, we saw the beanstalk, which had been there all along. We just hadn't noticed it up until this moment.

"Should we?" I asked.

"Think there's leprechauns up there?" he asked.

I laughed. "Maybe there's a jolly green giant." The beanstalk looked so very, very tall, and I was tired.

"Hey," Bobby said, "we don't have to rush into anything. It doesn't even have to be today. Maybe we could," he suggested. And our eyes turned toward the bed.

"Yeah," I said smiling. "I'd like that." But could we throw a blanket over this video monitor thing, just in case."

"Right," he said. "Good idea."

"And, after this, do you think we could wear the leaf

clothes? I mean I've always wanted to wear leaf clothes."

"Sure," he said. "And look for leprechauns?"

"Just no elves. I draw the line at elves."

"Understood," he said.

Together, we walked over to the bed, and I swear that I could smell the fragrant scent of pine needles.

The Expert Consultant from Amityville Gives Her Opinion on Your Second-Rate Haunted House

There are too many spiderwebs and not enough blood. Speaking of blood, did you use ketchup? Because no one uses ketchup anymore. It's too bright and too clumpy. And witches? While some are okay, most of them don't have that Romantic Era quality that you're looking for in a country manor attraction. Unless you live in Salem, witches just don't work. Think coiled executioners' ropes. I can show you how to make them pop out of the ceiling. Coffins are good, but vampires are so last season. Hire some children, too, preferably girls, preferably twins. Preferably sporting pigtails and blue jumpers. They should stay silent, but they can grin. For sound effects, you want creaking doors, howling wolves, eerie laughter, and screams that mimic the cries of the damned. As for props, vintage dolls do work well. So do rustic wooden crosses. Hang them upside down or sideways. Make them look askew. Put out some notched beeswax candles. Draw some pentagrams clockwise in chalk. Like this. Sprinkle around some white powder on the wood floors. Then walk through it in big-soled shoes. Cover the antique furniture with white sheets. Hang oval-shaped mirrors. For the dining room, put out some half-eaten food and lipstick-stained, not-quite-empty goblets. Oh, yes, of course, a Ouija board is always ominous, but don't let anyone touch it. Once the darkness is unleashed, it can't be contained. Remind me to tell you what happened to my brother. After he went on the asylum tour with amateurs who had gotten their certification online, he was never the same. Where are your old black and white photos? Didn't your ancestors pass theirs down to you along with their burial instructions? The most important thing is ghosts. Wait—is this place even actually haunted? Well, I can help. Come with me to the top of the staircase, where the railing is loose. Walk toward the air and keep going. At first, it's awful, but you'll get used to it. Eventually.

The Other Elizabeth

It started as a military operation. In order to better defend ourselves against fascism, we could send soldiers across The Great Divide.

But then private companies got involved, and that's when things got weird. Targeted ads started appearing on social media: *See your dead loved ones again across The Great Divide.* The Great Divide wasn't just a metaphorical term. It was a literal space bridge between our two universes. We called their universe Alt.world, and they called ours Other Earth.

To us, our world was the real universe, authentic and true. And they thought the same thing about theirs.

There were differences, of course. Each person was allowed to make his or her own decisions, and sometimes our other self did not make the same choices that we had.

There were even companies that allowed you to see The Road Not Taken and what happened if you took it. So even the Frost poem became literal.

People missed their dead husbands/wives, mothers/fathers, maybe pets the most.

It started with pets. The flyers. The pop-up ads. *See Sparky again!*

I could see the appeal. I kind of wanted to see my dead cat Fluffy. But she had died twelve years ago. And not everything that was done in one universe could be undone in another.

People, even if they shared the same names and DNA, could be different. In one universe, maybe your husband had quit smoking like he said he would. So he didn't die of lung cancer at the age of 55. It could go the other way as well. Maybe, instead of canceling her flight, your wife boarded that plane, the one that crashed. And maybe you wanted to see her again. If the other version of her crossed from Alt.world to our world, you could. In many cases, the arrangement was mutually beneficial. A dead loved ones' bad habits could easily be forgotten after death. But, if you had to live with him for fifteen more years, then his little quirks like never putting a new trash bag in after taking the garbage out or never recapping the toothpaste became a little less charming. So, often, it was a win-win for both groups.

Things could get messy, of course. If you had sex with Alt.world you's husband, were you really cheating, or did it just not count? Details needed to be worked out, and contracts needed to be signed. Of course, things could go badly. So you had to sign waivers. *In the event that things do not go as planned, we will not hold Happy Reunions responsible.*

What started out as a way to help people heal became something more. Businesses realized that there was money to be made, not just in grief but in pleasure.

Billboards started appearing in subways and on the interstate. *Spice up your sex life with alt you. Could you be what your bedroom is missing?*

It wasn't just about sex either. Some wanted to seek out their other selves for a spiritual or religious awakening. Wouldn't you like to see what's possible with your other self?

I never thought of myself as a conservative before, but when it came to this, I kind of felt myself sympathizing with the *Our World, Their World* group. Some people thought they were a cult. Admittedly their tactics were a little militant. They stood at The Great Divide with their handmade signs and their sloppy clothes and their searing eyes chanting things like: *Our Earth, Our People. Their Earth, Their People. Keep Segregation Alive.*

I would be the first to admit that their messaging could use some work. Like who on (either) earth thought it was a good idea to use the word *segregation* in a chant?

Some of the younger people were a little more media savvy. They had not just pamphlets but graphic novels about the dangers of inter-Earth travel.

There were some logistical issues of course. Like if both of the planets were Earth, were you technically even leaving? And, also, how did we know that some people hadn't been doing this for years? You know how sometimes you see a friend after a long absence, and that friend seems like a totally different person? Well, what if that friend actually was a totally different person, what if it was alt.friend?

I assumed that Jason and I wouldn't be affected by interEarth travel, at least not yet anyway. We were a young couple in our late twenties. Our parents and siblings were still alive as were most of our good friends. We hadn't yet had children, or even seriously discussed the possibility of it. Our jobs were fairly satisfying, as were our social lives. At least, that's what I thought at least. And I believed that Jason felt the same.

Until he came home one night after work with the flyer. The flyers were red and green and blue and tie-dyed looking as if the makers of them had just gotten home from a '70s psychedelic rave.

I had gotten home earlier that night, so I was making vegetarian stir fry on the wok when Jason burst in the door, his mood light and airy like the mindless pop song that was playing on the radio.

"Hey, Lizzy," he said, "how was your day?"

"Good," I said, "how was yours?"

This was our usual comforting after-work banter. Many nights, it was followed by a kiss. Other nights, it was followed by something a little more lingery.

But, that night, Jason skipped a kiss and went straight to the flyer. He pulled it out of the backpack he took with him on the train.

"Have you seen these?" Jason asked.

I was a little disappointed. I was hoping that tonight was going to be a lingering night, not one of those *let's discuss current social and political trends and then catch the evening news on MSNBC* nights. "Yeah," I said, hoping that Jason would notice my lack of enthusiasm for the topic and drop it.

But he either didn't notice or he chose to ignore my ambivalence. "Everyone at work is talking about them," Jason said as he stole a half-cooked snap pea and still didn't attempt to kiss me.

"Hmm," I said, "is that so?" Jason knew me well enough to know that that was my *can we talk about something else instead now please* signal.

"Yeah," he said, continuing, "people are saying it could be the biggest thing since the mass production of cell phones."

"Hmm," I said again, wanting to point out that a flyer and cell phones were not analogous. Instead, since I could tell that he wasn't going to drop it, I asked the question he had wanting me to ask all along, "what is it?"

The flyer wasn't just a flyer. It was an advertisement for a company that offered "life changing opportunities." To me, that language sounded corny and ridiculous, like something a telemarketer or televangelist would say to seal

49

the deal and lock in your commitment. The company was called LifeSwap, like the personal security company LifeLock. In fact, I think the naming pun was meant to make you trust them, but I didn't. LifeSwap, was, according to Jason, transformative. I was afraid to ask him how he knew. Was he in fact alt.Jason instead of my Jason, and had I just not noticed because he seemed the same to me? Jason, sensing my confusion, elaborated. "Mags and Matthew did it, and said it was the most amazing thing they've ever done."

Mags and Matthew were one of those annoying couples who looked alike, thought alike, and dressed alike to the point that you wondered if they were actually two separate people or if they had morphed into a unit. I dumped more hoisin sauce on Jason's stir fry than I knew he wanted just for spite and then purposely took the last Diet Coke and didn't offer to split it with him. When he opened the fridge and saw that there were no more cans, he sheepishly admitted that he had meant to tell me that we were out and ask if I could pick some up on my way home from the college where I worked as the Assistant to the Assistant Dean of Student Life. It was a job that involved easy tasks, interesting interactions, and good benefits. I could do it during the day and work on my screenplays at night. I was working on one about a professor who turned into a rabbit and enjoyed his hare life so much that he didn't want to go back to teaching. Jason tried to act like he supported my work, but I think he thought that writing was just a phase I was passing through and eventually I would move on up in the world of college administration and become assistant to the provost or get a side gig selling real estate that would turn into my full-time job. "I can get some more Diet Coke tomorrow," I said, hoping that Jason would stop talking about this stupid flyer for this stupid company. But I knew he wouldn't because Jason was an adrenaline junkie. He has jumped out of planes, scaled rocks, and eaten foods that came with medical warning signs. I felt like this was a test. Would I be willing to try this next thrill rush him, or was I too tame? I imagined a future with Jason, so I caved and said, "Okay, tell me more."

LifeSwap, according to their virtual reality–like website, was a company that helped people reach their greatest potential by allowing them to unlock (that stupid pun again) a future that was beyond their wildest imaginings. Jason starred mesmerized at the Jetson looking couple on the computer screen as he jabbered on about how Mags and Matthew said that getting to know their other selves helped deepen their commitment to each other. "Isn't that what you want for us, Lizzy?"

I said I needed time to think. But Jason wouldn't let the idea go, so three days later, we were sitting in a video conference room listening to a presentation given by a woman with marshmallow white hair and green eyeliner, who I think was meant to look modern and enticing but instead looked like she was auditioning for a role in the next *Frozen* film. What would her cartoon character name be? Jana? Elsa and Anna were taken, but it felt like her character's name also needed to end with an *a*. By the end, Jason was singing the praises of LifeSwap as enthusiastically as a Mormon missionary. I was just along for the ride. In our couples counseling session (why did LifeSwap use therapeutic language, I wondered, when what it seemed like what it was actually selling was a fantasy, not

51

a solution, a chance to be another you), it was determined that Alt.world Lizzy and I would change places first. Then Jason and Alt.world Jason would trade places once our cycles were complete so that each of us could experience both worlds. To me, what it seemed like they were asking us to do was participate in a modernized version of a 1970s key party: trade husbands, trade houses, trade lives for seven to ten business days. (Weekends were negotiable.) Jason was all for it, but I had my doubts.

Alt.world Lizzy, who went by Beth, and Alt.world Jason were married. So that at least was encouraging. If they could take it to the next level as a couple, then why couldn't we? Beth was a performance artist and feminist theorist who had made a fortune when a commercial developer had wanted to acquire the lot where her grandmother's house had once sat. In my world, the house was still a house, and no such commercial development existed. In Alt.world, Jason was a bonds trader who really wanted to spend his days writing piano solos. But he chose practicality over pursuing his dreams. Plus, he felt like he owed it to Beth, who had bought their unnaturally large house and paid for their dozens of unnecessary servants. "Why do you pay a man to wash your dishes," I asked him, "when you could just load them into that huge perfectly functioning dishwasher?" Because, he explained, it's what Beth wants. Alt.world Beth seemed to get everything she wanted, from fresh squeezed orange juice each morning to the best parking spot on campus each afternoon to a perfectly chilled glass of white wine made with the finest local grapes each evening. Maybe, when I met her for our debriefing in two weeks, I would ask Beth for some tips. I wasn't really comfortable doing performance art or lecturing undergrads on feminist theory, so I spent my first Monday as Beth being fake sick. As fake sick Beth, I examined her plants and her emails. Her plants were succulents. And I wondered if this was because she didn't like to care for things or if she just wanted to be trendy. From her emails, I learned that Beth was very, very popular. I thought that maybe I should check on my Jason just to make sure he was handling Hurricane Beth okay. But when I called him that afternoon, he said that he was busy.

"Busy doing what?" I demanded. Jason hesitated then said he was making dinner plans with Alt.world Beth, who didn't like to cook. I was in no mood to go out to dinner with Alt.world Jason, so instead I offered to cook for him.

"Beth never cooks," he told me. He wasn't even sad or disappointed, just resigned like he had accepted her in all her beauty and brokenness. Did my Jason feel the same about me?

The next day, I decided to embrace my inner Bethness. After all, we were both Elizabeth. So I went to the college and taught her classes and flirted with strange men, in the way that I imagined that Beth would. It was all very liberating and satisfying and strange. But, at the end of the day, I was ready to go back to being Lizzy. So I texted Jason to see if he wanted to swap back. And I got no response. The next morning, Jason tried to call me at 7 a.m. But Alt.world Beth didn't get up at 7 a.m. so neither did I. He called me five more times. But I was busy eating the breakfast that my own personal Uber driver had brought me, and I wasn't about to interrupt that just to hear Jason's lame excuses. Finally he texted me: *Lizzy, we need to talk*. Instead of calling, I texted, *About what?* For a while, there was nothing. Then he finally typed: *I think we should extend the swap*. I wasn't in the mood to handle his request in a mature adult manner, so I turned my cell phone off and emailed Alt.world Jason to tell him that we should go out that night to a piano bar, so that I could hear him play. *Okay*, he emailed back, without argument, because he was used to being bossed around by a woman who looked like me.

I let Beth's Jason choose the restaurant where we went out to dinner. If Beth didn't cook, then I wouldn't either. At least not for one night. I enjoyed cooking, at least sometimes. Jason picked a steak place. I was pleased to discover that Jason was kind of his own man. Beth claimed to like matcha, which Jason and I agreed tasted like dirt, and fruit smoothies.

"I know vegetarianism is supposed to be better for the planet, but I just can't shake the meat habit," Jason said as if he were a secret heroin addict.

"I know what you mean," I said, as I cut into a dangerously undercooked piece of filet and felt like a criminal.

I paid for the meal with Beth's credit card. Afterward, we went to a jazz bar where Jason was like a poor man's Billy Joel. The bar didn't pay him in anything other than free drinks, but he was okay with that, and so was I. We could get whatever we wanted, and everyone thought I was Beth. An old man at the bar said he liked what I had done with my hair, and I flirted with him mercilessly. And then he told Jason he had caught himself a wild one, and we laughed and laughed, and then we started kissing and didn't stop.

A couple of days later, Other Earth Jason texted me and said he was ready to swap back. But the terms of the contract were clear. Both parties had to agree to the swap. That morning, I called my new Jason at the investment company where he worked and asked if I could have Beth's number changed. When he asked why, I said no reason, but I think he knew. "We should talk, Lizzy," he said. "Sure," I said, "just tell me when and where."

Jason chose his favorite restaurant, the one where he had proposed to Beth, and I felt like a contestant on *The Bachelor*. Would he choose Elizabeth number one or Elizabeth number two? Dinner was pleasant, but I didn't think anything had been decided.

Afterward he asked if he could take me to the mall. I said sure thinking that he wanted to buy me some lingerie, so that we could continue our kinky courtship. Instead, he took me to the jewelry store where he held my hand and called me "sweetie" and made it clear that we were a serious couple.

The salesman, sensing a live target, moved in for the kill. "Are you looking for an engagement ring for the lady?" he asked.

"No," Jason clarified. "She lost her wedding ring. It fell down a sewer grate, and we need to get a replacement."

The salesman looked at Jason and then he looked at me as if he couldn't figure out how to peg us. Jason was wearing a suit that looked very Wall Street. Meanwhile, I was wearing a Target T-shirt and jeans. Finally, he asked Jason if there was any particular price range that he had in mind. Jason gave him a withering look.

"She can have anything she wants."

When the salesman attempted to clarify, Jason simply

repeated "anything." The salesman attempted to show us $25,000 rings, but I brought him down a few price brackets. I couldn't see spending that kind of money on a hunk of metal, even if it was considered to be precious.

After that, Jason took me to the mall food court for some Ben & Jerry's. No smoothies for us, he said. It was wedding week.

"But we're not," I began.

"Aren't we?"

"What's your driver's license number and your social security number and your date of birth?" he asked.

I told him, and he told me that they were the same as Beth's. But why are our phone numbers different, I asked.

Phone numbers, he said, aren't unique identifiers, and they can change over time.

I could see that he had given this a lot of thought, so I asked him, "Whose idea was the swap?"

"It was other world Jason's," he said. "He reached out to her. And then she approached me."

"When she approached you," I asked carefully as I took a bite of my waffle cone and tried not to get ice cream on my arm, "were you reluctant?"

"I would have given her anything," he said as he wrapped his tongue around a bit of brownie. "But it did give me pause when I realized she was willing to trade me in so easily. So when LifeSwap reached out with the contract, I read it cover to cover, including all fifteen pages of disclosures. And it turns out that she can't come back to this life, this earth, unless we all agree, and I don't."

"But doesn't it feel a little wrong to you to be living off her money, in her house?"

"Not really, he said, "should it when she was willing to sign it and me away so easily?"

"I don't know," I admitted.

Jason asked if I wanted to go to the cell phone store.

I said I need a few days, to think about it.

He nodded. "I'll do whatever you want, Lizzy."

"Let's go home," I said. Wondering if *home* was the right word. And I went to Beth's house and slept with Beth's husband.

I wondered if, the next morning, I would feel the kind of regret that many of my students did after staying out the night before drinking and waking up embarrassed by the memory of their twilight wildness, but I didn't. I felt good. I felt happy. And I wondered if Jason felt the same.

"Any regrets?" I asked as I kissed him and then put on my teacher clothes to go play dress up Beth.

"None," he said. "You?"

"Not many," I admitted.

I checked my voicemail. Other World Jason had left me 47 messages. I listened to one, and it was so whiny and annoying that I deleted all the rest. This life had begun to feel real, and that life had begun to feel like a distant memory. I texted my new, improved Jason and said I was ready to go to the cell phone store later if he was. He said, okay, if I was sure. While we were changing our numbers and leaving no new information about how to reach us, I asked him if he was going to quit his day job.

"I've been thinking," he said, "that maybe I should keep it. In case we decide to have children."

"Oh, um, wow," I said.

"Too much, too soon?"

"Um, no, it's just." I felt like I could cry because I was so happy. I had a great husband, a great house, a great life, and all I had to do was swap earths to get it. "Maybe we could get a dog first? And," I hesitated before adding, "what about Beth?"

"Beth," he said, "is Beth, but you, Lizzy, are my wife now."

And just like that I became Alt.world Elizabeth. And I didn't look back.

Belonging

Claudine woke up panting, broken, not sure how to reattach the displaced bones. At first, she only had 206, like most of us, but it quickly became clear that the patrons in Row I needed more assistance than she could provide with just the factory warehouse number.

"I'll get right on that," she said in response to their request for extra seat cushions, not-too-cold ice water, and a fifteen-page color Sciatica brochure.

They looked so common in their khaki pants and pullover shirts. Who would have predicted they would be so Sunday matinee, penny candy diva asking for such odd extras but refusing to pay concession-stand prices? And then, of course, no tip.

In her mind then, she was reading a Ray Bradbury novel about Martians and gathering mint leaves by the backyard pond before the overzealous local mowers, who had also sliced a hole in the underground hose with their blades, plowed through the precious plants like they were run of the mill, even though it should have been clear that leaves are not weeds and hose line is not grass.

At least twenty of the original bones hurt. The new ones she felt less kinship with, since they were only temporary, transitory, hers for now on interlibrary bone loan, and if she didn't return them to the bone depository promptly by 8 p.m. Wednesday (that seemed an easy enough time to remember, still she set a Google calendar notification) her credit card would be charged $24.99 per bone. At thirty-two bones, the number was staggering. And, if she didn't get the bones back on time, her *needing it to get through the day* caramel latte would be a thing of history, like the artifacts found at the Lost Colony.

How do you lose over a hundred English settlers? How do you make what you can't keep feel like it should remain there for now, part of the school field trip tour group when it's really only that kid from the homeschooling co-op with the unruly hair and cracking lips, the one your mothers told you to include but you really never did because you knew then that even the spectacular visitors you can't keep, can't file and categorize the *here for the day gone tomorrow* along with the rest of the elementary aged kids? No matter how much you close your eyes and wish for thunder, the gods' failures aren't yours. You only have so many bones to break.

Ohio River Oracle

People liked to call it the town that time forgot. But it was more accurate to say we lived in a town that progress forgot. We used to be a bustling port city on the Ohio River. And then the mills closed down or mostly closed down, and the area's once-thriving pottery business could no longer support us all, and we weren't prosperous anymore. Or prosperous at all. Downtown was a mess of mostly boarded up storefronts. To call the town economically depressed was generous. Economically devastated was more accurate. Almost every day, in the paper, there was a story about another drug raid on the East End. Sometimes, it seemed like half the people in the town were on welfare or on drugs.

We were a town that people left, and, when they came back to visit old relatives or attend class reunions, they said it was even more depressing than they remembered. It's not as if we didn't have anything. We had a Wendy's, a McDonald's, even a new Dairy Queen. And then there were some local restaurants that had decent food and unpredictable service. One restaurant moved locations four times before it finally closed. You could make a living here, but it was hard. The best game in town was the hospital. So I worked as a CNA there at night and took college classes to become an RN at the local branch campus of Kent State during the day. Donnie worked at a factory. The lucky ones got out, went off to livelier places like Columbus and Cincinnati, but I stayed for the sake of Donnie who didn't want to leave his friends. He was optimistic that things would turn around.

Everybody knew everybody here like in some TV

show, but not everybody was nice. Some of us were freaks. In good and bad ways. Cassie Jones was one of us, one of them. Maybe you don't believe in this kind of thing, and, if not, that's okay. I'm not sure if I do either.

Cassie Jones was the local oracle. Or psychic, if you will. She didn't have a neon sign in some shop with a Giant Eagle and a Subway. People just went to her and paid her at her house, a run-down two-story thing. It was not too far from where I went to church, but off the beaten path. It wasn't somewhere you passed on your way to anywhere. Cassie didn't seem particularly troubled by her burdens. Lacking education and parents, telling fortunes was the way she made her living. And it was a good living, considering the other options.

Her prophecies were like anything, like a good luck charm, a four-leaf clover. Maybe they worked, maybe they didn't, but, in case they did, what was the harm in asking her? So when Donnie proposed to me, I went to see Cassie. We knew each other from way back. We had been to school together, all the grades until sophomore year, when she got pregnant the first time and dropped out.

When I went to see her that summer day, she did the usual. Wearing a white dress and some tacky costume jewelry necklace, she lit the four candles, each one representing the corners of the earth.

After lighting the candles, she spread out the cards on a little table. They were multicolored cards featuring labeled figures in contorted positions. My eyes teared up. Everything smelled like incense. Cassie looked up at me with her cats-eye marble blue eyes and said, "Joanie, you sure you want to do this?" The sound of her voice was reluctant but sweet.

I nodded. Her blonde hair was pulled back in messy

braids.

Cassie seemed tense.

"It's just a game, right?" I teased. I had come from work and was wearing my heart-covered hospital scrubs. She stared down at the cards with obvious displeasure. "Maybe we should quit while we're ahead," she suggested. Her seriousness seemed unnecessary, silly. "Cassie, quit stalling and tell me," I said. Just then, one of Cassie's kids peered round the corner. Some of the kids were hers. Some not. She was one of those women who seemed to be perpetually pregnant. No one talked about who the father or fathers were. No one really knew. In addition to the kids who were biologically hers, Cassie took in strays. I don't know what the logistics of this were. If she got any money from the state or if they just came to her, one lost child to another. All I knew was this. I'd heard that more than one prominent local official was seen pulling away from her house at odd times of the day and night. And she never seemed to have any trouble with the law though her car tags had expired years ago, and she didn't have any insurance that I knew of.

"The cards can be wrong, you know?" Cassie said. We were both twenty years old.

"What?" I demanded.

"They say murder," she said and then apologized, offered me some Diet Coke. I declined, said I had to go.

I left her house that day and avoided her for some time until one day, after Donnie and I had been married for about two years and everything going smoothly, I ran into Cassie at the Giant Eagle.

Cassie was over in the produce section, stomach bulging like a watermelon, lugging three dirt-covered little ones—one in the cart, two by her sides.

She was examining sweet yellow onions and trying to calm the kids who were pulling at her hippie skirt. She did know how to dress the part.

I was tempted to go then, leaving her there. Part of me wanted to put the sound of her crying kids behind me just as I'd done with her prophecy. But I remembered Cassie in better days. When we'd shared fruit roll-ups and traded secrets. Before her parents died and she'd started trading fortunes and God knows what else for money.

"Cassie," I said.

She turned. She looked tired and wary. The circles under her eyes looked like fight bruises.

"Joanie," she acknowledged.

Once again, I was tempted to turn, grab my frozen meals, and leave her amid the apples and oranges. But instead, I said, "What can I do to help?"

I saw the gratitude in her eyes. She handed me a half-dressed child in Pampers who appeared to be about one. "Could you hold her?"

I nodded. "When're you due?" I asked as Cassie tried to manage the two others, a boy and a girl. One appeared to be screaming about a sippy cup, another about some other unknown childhood woe.

"Soon," she said as if due dates and doctor's appointments were things that other people worried about. I wondered if she got medical care at all. But it was none of my business.

My mother, who worked in a hair salon one plaza over, liked to say, "God helps those who help themselves."

"You feeling okay?" I asked.

"Oh, yeah," she said, dazed. Clearly lying.

The red-headed girl would not be comforted. I offered

to trade Cassie one child for another, the baby for the toddler.

"She's going through a stage," she said. I tried to decide what to think of Cassie. At my church, they were always talking about sinning. The sin of lust. The sin of jealousy. I wasn't jealous of Cassie, and yet, it must be nice not to have to worry about working a regular job like the rest of us. *Yeah,* I said to myself after surveying her screaming kids, *nice. Don't be such a jerk, Joanie.*

"Hi," I said to the girl, who, as if by magic, stopped screaming when I picked her up.

"Thanks," Cassie said with relief and exhaustion, "You're really good with them."

"No problem," I said. "You know, we should talk again. I'm sure you're busy, but call me if you need anything, okay?"

I didn't really expect her to take me up on the offer. For as long as I'd remembered, she'd never asked me or anyone else for anything. After her parents died of some mysterious illness, she just kept to herself, told people's fortunes for money, food, and whatever else she traded for, and somehow scraped by.

It was my day off, and I was doing the laundry and dishes.

When I answered the phone, she said, "I'm bleeding, Joanie, real bad." At first I didn't even know who it was. And then I didn't know what to do.

"You want me to call 9-1-1?"

I knew after I'd said it that it was the wrong question. "I'll get Doc Flaherty. If he's not around, I'll drive you to the hospital."

Dr. Patrick Flaherty was a real character. A man who

still made house calls and acted like someone out of those Old West TV shows. Yet, he was everybody's family doctor of choice. There was him and everybody else. He had an actual office in a plaza with some local pizza place where they cooked the pizza but served the toppings raw, but half the time he was out making house calls, and nobody minded.

I knocked on Doc Flaherty's door. He was sitting down to Saturday dinner and his wife, a white haired schoolteacher-looking woman named Irene, said he couldn't be disturbed.

"This is an *emergency*," I said and barged on in.

"Why, Joanie, what on earth is the matter? Are you hurt? You look alright to me," said a surprised Doc Flaherty as he wiped the roast gravy off his white beard. Despite his age, he was still a handsome man.

"No, it's not me, but you gotta come with me. It's a matter of life or death!"

"Just calm down now, and tell me what's going on." I knew he was hoping I was being a hysterical woman, so he could get back to enjoying his roast beef. So instead of leaping to his feat like I'd hoped he would, he sat there and waited for me to explain.

I don't know why I did what I did next. I went over right next to him, and I said so low that only he could hear, "It's Cassie." I don't know why I'd whispered it, but I could tell from his reaction that my instincts had been right.

His face turned a shade a white then that I'd never seen before. He bolted out of his chair like a man on fire.

"What on earth is going on, Patrick?" Irene asked.

"I gotta go treat a patient; I'll explain about it later,

dear."

We both jumped into his pickup truck because Doc Flaherty said it would ride easier up to the back road hills out where Cassie lived. He also already had his medical supplies in the truck.

During the car ride, Doc Flaherty didn't say anything, didn't even try to make polite conversation. The only thing he said, toward the end when we were almost up the last hill was, "I didn't know you and Cassie were friends."

I didn't want to admit that we weren't really, that I wasn't any more privileged to her secrets than anyone else, so I just said, "Well, you don't know everything."

"No," he said in a sad tone that sounded like regret, "I don't. Far from it."

When we got there, Cassie's door was locked. I was about to suggest that we knock, but Doc Flaherty had already pulled out a key. I didn't ask why he had one, what that could mean. At the time, it really didn't seem to matter. I just followed him in. He was calling her name loudly.

One of the children, a boy with skin the color of milk chocolate, said, "Momma's in the bedroom on the floor."

Doc Flaherty was no young man. In fact, if I'd had to estimate, I would say he was at least sixty. However old he was, I knew he was a good deal older than me. So he surprised me when he ran up the steps so fast that I couldn't keep up. The little boy and I were both left staring up after him.

He yelled down, "Joanie, go get my medical kit." In all the excitement, he'd left it in the truck.

When I made my way up to her bedroom a few minutes later, as quickly as I could, lugging that leather bag, he was sitting next to her on the floor, looking scared as

67

hell, saying, "Don't you die on me, girl."

She wasn't moving at all.

Seeing me, he said, "Joanie, I'm glad you're here. You're going to have to help me get her on to the bed. I'm going to have to cut her open."

I looked at him wide-eyed and open-mouthed, "Shouldn't we take her to the hospital?"

"There's no time," he said, "if I don't operate now, she's gonna die. We've got to get this baby out of her."

He was so determined and certain that I did what he told me to do. He looked at her in such a way that I knew it wasn't just a patient that he'd be losing if Cassie died, but in that moment, I didn't care. I wanted to save her too.

Two hours later and covered in blood, Doc Flaherty looked over at me and said, "You did real good, Joanie, real good. I think she's gonna make it."

"I'm glad," I said, and I meant it. I realized that I cared about Cassie, too, though not as much as he did. Watching the tender way he smoothed her hair, I was almost certain that he was the father of at least one of them babies, maybe all. Or maybe he was more like a father to Cassie herself.

"Why don't you go clean up?" I suggested. "I can stay with her in case she wakes up."

"She should be out for a while," he said. "I gave her chloroform so she wouldn't wake up during the surgery."

The words *the surgery* surprised me still. Even though I worked at a hospital, I couldn't believe that he had operated on her right there on her bed and that I had helped. The baby was alive and being looked after by one of its many full- or half-sisters. They were used to caring for each other, from what I gathered.

Staring at Cassie then, I realized that I knew so much

more about her than I ever had before, and that none of it was verifiable or repeatable. I took Cassie's hand in mine while she slept and whispered, "Sis, it's going to be okay." I swear her mouth turned up a little like a smile, but maybe I just imagined that.

When Doc returned from cleaning up, he asked if I needed to get home to Donnie. "No," I said, "I can stay if she needs me."

"You go, I'll stay," he said in a way that meant he wanted me to leave. "I should be here anyway just to make sure there aren't any complications."

"Okay," I said and walked out the door. Once outside, I realized that I didn't have a way to get home since I'd left my car at his house. Even though it was a good mile to get to my car, I decided to walk it rather than go back in.

That next day, when Doc Flaherty called, I didn't explain to Donnie why he was calling or what this thing was about, I just said, "Look, a friend a mine's in trouble, and I gotta go."

Since the last time I'd seen Cassie in the Giant Eagle, Donnie had gotten laid off from his job at the factory. He was sitting on the couch drinking Miller Lite and watching the Steelers game. He looked at me with surprise then, like Doc Flaherty had, but his look was meaner. Alcohol made him mean. "What friends? Joanie, you and I both know you ain't got any friends. All you do is work and gripe at me to get off my ass."

"That shows what you know," I said. I was hurt, but I tried not to let him see it. I could tell him where I was going, but I didn't.

When I got to Cassie's, Doc Flaherty was still there.

He said, "I wanted to wait till you got here before I left." His eyes looked red, and his face looked tired.

"I'll take good care of her," I said.

"You're a good friend, Joanie." I was too ashamed to tell him how untrue that was because Donnie's words stung me still. Him saying I didn't have any friends. I realized that he was kind of right. There were people I talked to, but, in case of an emergency, who could I count on? I had Cassie, but Cassie was nice to everyone, even someone like me, who was suspicious of her motives.

Instead what I said, as I watched him put his coat and hat on and head home to his wife was, "She deserves better than both of us."

And then I walked upstairs as quickly as I could to see if Cassie was okay. When I got up there, she was lying in bed, awake but weak.

Her face brightened a little when she saw me. "Joanie," she said weakly, "thank you for helping me. Patrick says you saved my life."

Patrick, I thought.

"You should've just called him yourself, Cassie."

"But I couldn't," Cassie explained. "I promised that I never would."

Cassie, I realized, always kept her promises. I didn't press her for details. Instead, what I did was felt her forehead to make sure she didn't have a fever. Then I asked could I get her anything to eat.

"Oh, no, I'm not hungry, but check on the children, see if they need anything. They're scared to come in here and see me like this."

After that, after I proved my loyalty by not telling a soul about what I knew about Cassie and Doc Flaherty, she was as loyal as a sister. Cassie Jones would have done anything for me. But I didn't know then how far *anything* would go. I didn't know if Cassie was like the rest of us who say they'll do anything for a friend but only mean anything *within certain limits*.

Things weren't going so well with me and Donnie. He wanted me to have a baby, said that people were starting to talk, but I was worried about money. I felt like it made him feel better if I did what he wanted, but his meanness was starting to scare me. I didn't know if I wanted to have a baby, let alone get a dog, with him, unless he stopped drinking and stopped treating me so mean.

"Donnie, would you mind helping me clean up?" I said. His beer and cigarette butts were everywhere, and the house was a mess.

"Can't," he said. "I'm busy. Stop nagging me like a little bitch, woman."

"I don't appreciate being called a bitch," I said.

He got real close to me, and said, "Well, that's too bad because you fucking are." And then he hit me, his breath wreaking of alcohol. I was too stunned to do anything but stand there feeling dumbfounded.

"Hey, baby," he said, "I'm sorry, but you know you deserved it. You can't be disrespecting your man like that. Understand?"

I nodded because I didn't know what else to do, and then I went to the bedroom alone and shut the door.

As things worsened with Donnie, I started spending more and more time with Cassie. One afternoon as I was standing there on her front porch helping her watch her babies, Cassie said to me, "Joanie, if you ever need help with things at home, you let me know." She looked me right in the eyes, her bright blue eyes seeming to penetrate into my skull and the thoughts in my brain.

But I denied it at first, and I kept on denying it for a while. "What on earth are you talking about?" I said light and breezy. I turned from her. But it did no good.

Things with Donnie continued to get worse, and I wished I had listened to Cassie's warning. I was also a little mad at her because I wished she could have been more specific when she'd told me my fortune. That word she had said that day kept coming to me spelled out in typewriter letters: m-u-r-d-e-r. Finally, one afternoon while I was helping her hang laundry on the clothesline in the backyard, I broke down and asked her, "Cassie, what did you mean all those years back when you told me about Donnie?"

She stopped what she was doing, which was carrying a basket load of sheets from the porch to the outside and said, "I wish I could've been clearer, but that was all I could see back then."

"No, I mean, did you mean he would kill me, or?"

"Joanie," she said her tone serious, "if you don't do something soon, I think we both know which way this is heading."

Driving home, back to Donnie and misery, I realized that she was right. I had to do something.

What I finally did was I bought a gun. Cassie came with me. She knew a guy who knew a guy. As with everything Cassie did, who knew if it was registered or legal. Then Cassie showed me how to shoot. She had good aim. You could tell she'd had some practice.

"Joanie," she said, when I looked at the gun with fear,

"I'm only doing this for your protection."

On Thursday night, with Donnie drunk and hitting on me before seven o'clock, I'd finally had enough.

"I'm sorry you're having a rough time, but none of this is my fault."

"Don't back talk me, you stupid cunt. Don't act like you're too good to fuck me now."

I knew that he still wanted me to have a baby. But I knew by now that that was no solution. I wasn't sure anymore, after watching Cassie and all her kids, if I wanted to have children at all. Maybe I should have just let him have his way.

"I'm not going to fuck you when you're acting like this," I said, though I knew it was stupid as soon as the words were out of my mouth. Donnie came after me then, murder in his eyes. I tried to run, but he followed me right up the stairs. He was surprisingly fast for being so drunk. That was when I went for the gun, a Smith & Wesson .38 special. He didn't know where I had it hidden or even that I had it at all. But I kept it loaded back in a corner in the closet right under some sweaters. He never did laundry, and I knew he'd never think to look through my clothes. Desperation gave me the strength to outrun him. I locked the door and got out the gun. When he bashed the door in, I was standing there, waiting with the revolver in my hands. "What the hell?" he asked, wide-eyed. I tried not to think of the way Donnie had looked on the day of our wedding, back when he'd been so confident and handsome. I had surprise on my side, and I squeezed the trigger, once and then again. I heard the sound of the gunshots, watched Donnie fall onto the wood floor hard. "Joanie, you—" I wondered if he was going to say something loving. I felt

73

bad for him, went to take his hand, but he grabbed me and tried to strangle me by the neck, said, "Fuck you, you stupid bitch," and then I shot him good and dead. He didn't move again, but I poked him just to be sure. Afterward, I sat there shaking. Finally, I thought to call Cassie. I was convinced I'd go to jail for life.

Cassie was calm. "Don't touch anything," she said, "I'll be right there."

Cassie showed up at the door free of all her children. She told me she'd parked on the curb.

"Go take a shower as fast as you can. I'll handle the rest. Just don't wash your hair. You don't want it to look like you just took a shower. Take your clothes and put them in a trash bag. Bury them under something else then drive them to the dump. Once you've left, I'll call the police. The only thing is," she began.

"What?"

"I've got to tell them I killed him."

"How do you know they'll believe you?"

"The police chief is a friend of mine," she admitted.

I wasn't surprised.

"Won't there be traces of blood or something?"

"It won't matter," Cassie said.

Cassie had a look of determination on her face that scared me. I didn't ask what she was going to say.

"You need to know, and I hate this, but we won't be able to see each other for a while now. Because of what I'll have to tell them. Joanie, if you hear things about Donnie and me, I just want to make sure you know better than to believe them."

I did, of course, know better, but I couldn't help wondering. Had Cassie been honest with me? Had she been honest with anyone?

I didn't see her very often after that. I couldn't. Because what they told me was that Cassie had killed my husband in self-defense. They told me she and Donnie had been lovers.

"How do you know she wasn't lying?" I asked, surprised that everyone was so willing to take her word.

"Ma'am," the police officer said, "I'd rather not say. Sometimes it's better that way."

"Yes," I agreed. For a moment, I had forgotten the truth—that I had killed him.

We didn't speak for a while, Cassie and I, not even after she'd been tried and acquitted. Some of the things she said about Donnie at the trial, some of the things she knew, it made me wonder. Wonder if other women avoided her for the same reasons I did. It came out at trial that she knew about the scar on Donnie's inner right thigh and how he sometimes would call out for you in moments of unbelievable tenderness, moments that made you wanna forget how bad he could be all the rest of the time, and he'd say, "Oh, Momma, oh Momma, you sure know how to love me." It made me question if maybe one of those children could've been his. Even though, as far as I know, the only time he really went out toward the end was to get more beer. Still, I remembered how I'd felt when she said that at the trial and all the women in the town were talking about it to one another, whispering "poor thing," and I felt so bad I could barely stand it. I reddened and wondered why I'd ever trusted her, didn't know if I could ever forgive her for embarrassing me like that. Maybe she just knew these things about Donnie because she could see them. But how could I be sure? But then a funny thing happened, time passed, and I began to miss Cassie because she was the best friend I'd ever had, but I couldn't see her out in public because of the way things had ended between us. So one night, I drove out toward her house, waited till the last car left, then I walked up to her porch and knocked on the door.

"I'm closed," she said.

"I thought you didn't ever close," I said through the screen. The night was hot and humid like something out of a murder mystery movie, and Cassie didn't have air conditioning. For a moment, it was so quiet I could hear the chirp of the crickets.

She had her back turned and hadn't looked up when I'd knocked. Did she know it was me when she told me to go? If so, I couldn't really blame her. I'd hung her out to dry, I guess.

"Cassie, it's Joanie," I said because I wasn't about to leave without trying.

"Joanie?" she asked without turning, as if she was afraid to hope.

"Yeah."

"Well, come in, I guess," she said and got up slowly. She was as big as an animal at the zoo, pregnant again. Oh, God, I thought. I wondered sometimes if she's slept with every man in that town under the age of 95. But I tried to stop having these thoughts.

"Who's the father, Cassie?" I asked her with uncharacteristic bluntness.

She didn't answer, just asked, "Do you want me to put on some water for tea?"

"Do you even know?" I asked the air because I knew she wasn't going to tell me. "About Donnie," I began, and she stopped dead.

"I'm tired, Joanie," she said.

"It's all the same to you, isn't it?" I asked, though I hadn't come there to be mean.

Cassie's face turned white, and I could tell I'd hurt her, even though I hadn't meant to. Maybe I'd been wrong. I didn't think I'd ever know for sure. She turned toward the stairs. But I stopped her.

"Hey, how you holdin' up?" I asked.

"You know," she said.

"I don't," I said because I'd never really understood.

Cassie lifted up the hem of the long skirt she was wearing. "My legs are swelling pretty bad this time."

"Does it hurt?"

"You can get used to lots of things," she said.

"Like having everybody in town think you're a murderess?"

Her eyes widened. "Joanie, I don't want to fight. Stay or go. I'm going to bed."

"You got me out, Cassie. Why not yourself?"

We stood there for a long time.

"Your feet look painful; sit down. I'll make the tea, okay?"

Cassie nodded. And then I asked again while I had the courage, "You love him?"

She didn't answer, but I knew then what the silence meant. And I felt, of all things, relief.

Water, power, danger

They said don't go in the water. But I was never one to follow rules, take advice, or color within the lines.

The warning signs were everywhere. On the road. At the beach. Right along the shores.

Danger! Turn back. Enter at your own risk.

The lifeguard chairs were unmanned. The beaches uncluttered by towels and chairs and humans.

In a way it was beautiful, the only life the creatures of the sea. Clams and snails and fish and crabs. As well as those monsters unseen.

But I wasn't afraid of monsters. I had already faced so many down.

Plus there was the siren song, the water luring, and I could not resist.

There were other signs of distress. The clothes washed up, shapeless, on the beach. The cars in the parking lot that looked like they'd been sitting for days or weeks. As with anything, not everyone who enters would return.

But I was cocky, confident. I would take my chances.

I was undeterred by the man who rose up from the sand to warn me.

"Miss," he said. "I'm sure you've heard."

"Yes, yes," I said, impatiently, dismissively, for I had been answering the call for days.

"I drove here from the part of the state where there is no water."

He nodded sadly.

"Yes," he said. "I suppose someone has to sacrifice herself. If you're sure." Then turtle man went back to hiding in the sand.

There are so many interesting animals that exist on the edge of land and sea. Most will never see them because they don't know where to look.

I stripped down to my skin and walked slowly steadily into the water's warm welcoming embrace. But part of me resisted. I was doing what he wanted now, and I hated that he could demand, and I'd respond. He was merciless, and he did not hesitate to use my affection for humans against me.

"If I do this," I said, "will you let the others go?"

The sea king nodded, but I needed proof.

The ocean released them. Gasping, horror stricken, they emerged with blue-tinted skin and soaking clothes. Looking a bit like zombies, they seemed crazy grateful.

"It was you that they wanted," an old man said.

I nodded. The sound of my voice now that I was in the water, would shatter them.

But silently I corrected him. Not them, but him. My father demanded his price, my freedom. If I didn't return, the humans would suffer. He was so tiresome and tyrannical as fathers of daughters often are.

"Ariel," a young boy whispered, "your father is waiting."

I nodded again and turned away. I didn't want him to see my tears.

I wished I had told Eric goodbye. The farther I walked, the more I would change. Legs to fins, lungs to gills.

I would become my sea self, triumphant and trapped.

But underwater rumbling, my father would hear my voice, and one day, maybe not for another hundred years, and maybe not with this prince but another, my father would let me live life free.

The Great Escape

They told us we didn't have anything to fear. But they were rich and privileged, and what they knew of monsters could be hidden, buried, or made to disappear. Like the lost DNA sample in the Dawson case. We all knew who killed that girl. But the DNA was the only physical evidence. And another woman vouched that Frankie was with her the whole entire night. The woman who was Frankie's alibi feared the Hyde family more than she feared the penalties of perjury.

They were the richest and most destructive family in the county. We just hoped that no one would put any fool ideas into Beau's head to run for office. It was when local yokels went national that all their petty and not so petty crimes tended to be exposed and embarrass the towns they came from. Rich people anywhere were like rich people everywhere. But it made big city folks feel better to mock our rich weirdos even though they had their own.

The weather had just started to turn cool when everything started, and we didn't think anything of it, at first. We thought it was just boys looking for excitement, girls wanting boys' attention, or old men watching girls they couldn't have.

It had been a hot but uneventful summer, aside from Marjorie running off with that inappropriate older man from two towns over. Her father found out, threatened the man with a shotgun, and brought her back home. It was clear that she didn't want to be back, and we didn't blame her. We all knew her father.

One day, while Marjorie was putting price stickers on

packs of ramen noodles and cans of red beans at her father's store, I summoned up the courage to ask her what it was like out there, out in the world beyond Reedsville.

"The sky looks the same, the air smells the same, but everything feels different," she said. And I could tell that she wished she were anywhere but here.

But ever since she left, or tried to leave, her daddy was watching her closely, and upon seeing her talking to me, a normal high schooler with friends who had never shown any interest in his loner daughter before, he gave her a strong look.

Though she was only in her late teens, early twenties, she looked old around the eyes. As if this town had swallowed her whole, and she was just trying to figure her way out of the belly of the whale. Before I walked away, I whispered, so low that only she could hear, "Maybe you could try again."

She seemed surprised. When her daddy turned away, she nodded slowly, with just a hint of a grin on her face. I smiled, a big bright smile, and then I proceeded to the register with five Kit Kats and two cans of Cheerwine. I knew that if you came into the store, you had to buy something or Marjorie's Dad, Big Joe, would call the police on you for loitering.

While the deputy sheriff, who was a distant relation to the Hyde's but not an entitled prick like the rest of the family, had tried to tell Joe that it wasn't a requirement for people to buy something from the store and that it wasn't illegal to browse, he would still feel obligated to respond to Joe's waste of time and waste of police resources calls, and I didn't want Big Joe to tie up my afternoon like that. I had crazy cousins to check on and stray dogs to feed.

I went to feed the dogs first because I liked dogs better

than I liked people. I mean, who didn't? Well, I guess some people didn't. What I liked about dogs was that dogs didn't lie to me. They didn't pretend to like you to your face then gossip about you behind your back.

After I put our dry kibble and water for the pack, which was basically just any dogs who needed it, I started making the rounds on the cousins. I began with the most difficult one first, Daisy Mae. Her mother had given her a tacky country girl name, and names have power. She had been beautiful at first, desirable, and lustful. She wanted and she took. Food, wine, men. And then she got fat, with hips the size of ancient tree trunks, and all that was left was the food and the alcohol. She used her disability check to go to the store and buy bread and lunch meats. Afterward, she fried up bologna and took a long slow puff of the cigarettes she'd splurged on. She had to make them last.

Daisy Mae was the first to mention what she called the faceless men, but because she believed in all sorts of unreal things, I didn't pay her rantings any mind. Why would I? In the past, she had told me about tree people, lightening snakes, and invisible mountains. The faceless men seemed no different. It seemed like another thing she had invented to add-some-excitement to her run of the mill life. And who could blame her? I didn't. I cleaned her toilets, swept her floors, and took out her trash. As I went to leave, she said, "You be careful out there, Madelyn."

"I always am," I said.

"Be extra careful," she said, with concern in her eyes.

"I will, Cousin Daisy."

"Come here and give me a hug." I did, and, in that moment, the girth and width of her was comforting rather than distressing.

The next cousin I went to visit was younger, Billy Joe.

But something had gone wrong with him, something that happened either when his mama was pregnant with him or not long after he was born. We were never sure, and we still loved him, but we didn't like to leave him too long by himself because we didn't want him to get any strange notions into his head. He was living in his mama's house even though she had left for work one day and had never come back and poor Billy was out there all alone. We knew that she had planned it because she had packed him five days' worth of peanut butter and jelly sandwiches and labeled them by day. He was halfway through with them when a neighbor went to check on him because she hadn't seen or heard his mama's car in days. She found him at home watching *Tom and Jerry* cartoons while a stack of dishes piled up in the sink. She called the sheriff, who called Aunt Jerry, who called me. And that's when I added him to my list of cousins to check on. With Billy, I always had to knock loudly on the door before entering because he was a big boy and tall, and I didn't want to run the risk of scaring him. "Billy, it's me, Maddie," I said as I banged. "I'm coming in." Billy was sitting in a corner hugging himself. He said he was scared of the people with the flat faces. I told him that people with flat faces couldn't see or breathe or eat, so he didn't need to be afraid. I made him boxed macaroni and heated up a can of green beans for him on the stove. When I left, he seemed more calm. I turned on Nick Junior for him on the TV since *Tom and Jerry* was over, so he wouldn't feel like he was alone.

After stopping to see Billy, I headed to Cousin Duke's. He was an eccentric old man who kept his house hot in the summer and cold in the winter and only flushed the toilet after every five uses to help keep the cost of utilities low.

When I got there, it was too warm inside even though we were in the process of passing from summer to fall and the weather had lately been in the 70s rather than in the 90s, but Duke was keeping himself cool by drinking ice water and fanning himself with a paper fold-up fan. "How's it going?" I asked, and I expected him to say same old, same old, but instead he gave me some apocalyptic answer. "We're at the end of the world, Maddie. How does it feel?"

"Like a Thursday," I replied. Duke said he didn't need anything, but he'd be seeing me soon, and I wondered what he meant, since I didn't plan to see him for a week. But being agreeable seemed easier than arguing, so I simply said okay.

My next stop was Juanita's house, and unlike the rest of my crazy cousins, she had been doing mostly okay for a long time. Even after her husband of fifty years died, she had managed. Things took a turn for the worse though after her lover died. She had always liked him better than her husband anyway maybe because she never had to live with him. I entered the living room of her trailer to find her sitting in her recliner, drinking ginger ale out of a plastic cup.

"You seem chipper, Maddie," she observed.

I nodded. Overall, it had been a good day, I thought.

"I take it that you haven't seen the scarecrow men, then?" she asked. I had been to visit four cousins, and all of them had mentioned that they felt like something weird was going on.

Was there some kind of network for the weird that they were getting their information from? Or.

"When did you see them?" I asked. "And what did they look like?"

Juanita took a sip of her ginger ale and offered me a cookie from a fresh sleeve of vanilla wafers. Even though I wasn't a fan of vanilla anything, I took it because I didn't want to risk offending her.

"If you'd seen them, Maddie, you would know."

I debated what to do next. Should I check in on the next cousin or look up information about these weird men online? In the end, I decided to go to the next house. Even if something strange was happening, I still needed to make sure all my cousins were okay.

Bob, Joe, and Vonda, the last three on my list, all mentioned some variation of monsters or messed up men, so I thought maybe I should listen up and pay attention. Sometimes, the isolated among us notice things that the rest of us are too busy to see. Joe said we better head out. When I asked how, he said he would give Daisy Mae a call. I thought that before I did anything I should run home and check on my mother. She was having one of those spells where she couldn't get out of bed. These came and went ever since I could remember. I didn't know if they'd started before or after my father left. I didn't know how to tell her about the men with messed up faces, so I simply said, "Mom, we've got to go. Or we might die here."

She heard me, but she barely moved, simply saying, "You go, Maddie. I was always going to die here." I knew what she said was true, so I didn't try to argue. Instead, I gathered up a couple of things that seemed like they might be helpful: deodorant, a toothbrush, my cell phone charger, a water bottle, a sweatshirt, some beef jerky, trail mix, five clean pairs of underwear. I didn't know if this was how you were supposed to pack for the apocalypse. Before I headed out, I gave Daisy a call. I wanted to make sure Joe had reached her. When Daisy answered, she was huffing and puffing, as if she had been climbing a flight of stairs.

"Oh, hey, Maddie, I'm just firing up the camper," she said. "I'm going to start rounding up the cousins."

"Okay, great," I said, though, in truth, I was surprised to hear that thing still worked.

"Well, if you need anything, you just let me know."

"Likewise," I said.

I threw my bag in the trunk and began to head slowly out of town. I was a little sad though because while I was glad that the cousins were maybe making it out, I felt terrible that I had left my own mother in our house to rot. I turned on some easy listening music and began to drive toward the edge of town. Just as I was about to make the turn toward Route 11, I slammed on my brakes. I saw one of my dogs, the beagle I called Prairie, and stopped to load her in my car. Oh my God, the dogs, I thought. I can't just leave the dogs. I also couldn't fit them in my mother's 2015 Toyota Corolla. As a Hail Mary, I called Cousin Daisy, and asked her if she could fit a few. She said they had room. And she would do her best. As I overthanked her, she said it was the least she could do.

"See you on the other side, Maddie," she said.

"See you on the other side," I said, hoping we both would make it.

As I approached the last diner on the way out of town, which was oddly, or not so oddly, featuring a last supper special, traffic had begun to back up. Just beside the line of cars, I saw Marjorie on foot, pulling a pink suitcase on wheels. I rolled down my window. "Hey, Marjorie," I said,

"Want a ride?"

She shrugged, and Prairie jumped in the back seat to make room.

As we waited in the line of cars heading out, I saw three strange things. One was the faceless men. They seemed to be headed into town by the hundreds. They had mannequin faces but normal arms and legs. They wore black suits and bowler hats.

The second strange thing was the Hyde family. They were attempting to cut in line in their fancy vehicles because they weren't used to following the same rules as the rest of us. But no one would let them in. Randy, who worked at the post office, even gave them the finger.

The third strange thing was that not everyone leaving was making it out. At the intersection of 254 and 11, someone, apparently one of the faceless men, had set up a checkpoint.

A vehicle three cars ahead of us didn't make the cut. We watched in horror as the occupants' faces seemed to melt off and their spirits lifted into the sky. Kind of like how it happened to those jerky people in that first Indiana Jones movie.

The next car made it out without a hitch.

"What do you think the criteria for this is?" I said to Marjorie.

Marjorie responded by quoting something that I thought was from the Bible. It made me wish I had paid more attention in Sunday school. "On account of the ten," she said. "I will not destroy it."

When it was our turn, I half expected our faces to melt off, but the faceless man at the check point just waved us through. Prairie howled her approval. Instead of racing down 11 as quickly as I could, I pulled over to the side of the road. This might be a long drive. So I thought maybe I should get out something to eat. I offered Marjorie some beef jerky. Just as I was about to head back onto the highway, I saw Daisy's camper approaching the checkpoint. I waited because I had to know. I breathed a sigh of relief as Daisy wheeled that massive bus-like monstrosity onto 11. Daisy saw me and gave me a thumbs up. To my relief, the dogs barked a greeting. And Prairie returned their hellos with a happy howl. To Marjorie, I said with pride and happiness, "That's my family." She just nodded. I told Marjorie she could change the radio channel. I expected her to say that whatever I wanted was fine. But, instead, she hit the scan button and stopped channel surfing when she got to the rap station. So we headed out of town to the music of Sir-Mix-A-Lot. I didn't know where we were going. But I felt like, wherever it was, we would survive.

Close to You

Jenny wasn't sure when she fell in love with the homeless man, who panhandled on Greenville Avenue near the Lowe's and the Walmart, but she thought it was between Jay and Ray. He was sensible, that homeless man. He had chosen a good spot.

But it could have been after Barry and before Mark. After a while, all the men blended together like melting M&Ms. Jay was the guy who worked at GameStop and constantly talked about leveling up. It was cute at first, but after a while she understood why he was still living in his mother's basement and wondered if he'd ever leave. Ray, on the other hand, was a serious jazz musician who lectured her about why all the music she listened to was trash. One day, when she found him editing her workout playlist to include better quality songs, she knew that the music between them had died. But before they broke up, she changed all his car radio presets to Top 40 stations.

The homeless man wasn't pushy, but he also wasn't passive. Unlike Jay the gamer, he wasn't satisfied with his lot in life. But, unlike Ray the trumpeter, he didn't ridicule her hair, her car, her records. When she brought him a Whopper junior, he didn't tell her that her tastes were too mainstream. But he also didn't just take what she gave him and like it. He asked for fries next time. She brought them as well as a Coke.

Barry was a fitness nut who didn't believe in drinking soda, so, when she dated him, she drank Dr. Pepper four times a day till her teeth started to hurt. When her gums began to bleed, she knew it was time to pack up her sugar and move on. Mark was a single father of a nine-year-old and the poster boy for wholesomeness. But he was so busy coaching Little League and helping his son earn merit badges that he didn't have time to see her. Unlike the homeless man. The homeless was at the intersection on schedule Monday, Wednesday, Friday, noon to three rain or shine. She knew she could find him when she needed him.

What Remains

Sometimes, she wanted him to die. And then he had. What she didn't expect was for his rotting corpse to stalk her.

She'd be going out to coffee or for a lunch date, and she'd see it, shedding fingers, toes, looking all *Tales from the Crypt* yuck.

After a while, she'd pretend she didn't see it. And then it would move to wave its bony hand. And she couldn't not see a skeleton waving its phalanges at her.

Last Wednesday, there she was, sitting in the corner by the $675 splattered paint on wall by local artist installation when she saw it, approaching from the entrance and using the handicapped button to help it because without muscles it no longer had a strong grip.

"Why," she had wondered out loud to the barista, "can't you kick that thing out?"

But the barista, who had recently completed her company mandated diversity training, had looked at her horrified, "That would be discriminatory," she said.

Couldn't they just amend the sign outside the door to read *No soul, no shirt, no service?* But that, the barista had noted, might offend the Wall Street bankers.

Alyssa had sighed and settled down to sip her bitter but not burned artisan coffee, tasting notes of hazelnut, witch hazel, and tree bark. It was so subtle and so earthy, she thought, smiling. Then she thought she smelled actual dirt, and she looked up, and there it was, dragging a trail of graveyard soil behind it.

Seriously, she thought, it has to be some kind of health and safety violation to have a corpse walking around in an area where food and drink were served. Why doesn't anyone else seem concerned?

A middle-aged man at a nearby booth with glasses, an expanding waste line, and a receding hairline gave her a sympathetic nod. "We all have our corpses to bear," he said. That annoying allusion to religion gave her an idea. She would head to the local Catholic Church and pick up some holy water.

She went to Saint Peter's because it was 0.6 miles away and she could walk it. She had been sitting too much at work anyway, and she needed to get in more steps.

As luck would have it, the church was open because they had just had a funeral, and they hadn't yet locked back up. So Alyssa went on in through the side entrance. She was standing in the vestibule trying to figure out how to pour the holy water from the font into her Klean Kanteen (the mouth wasn't wide enough to make it easy) when she ran into Father Brian a.k.a. Brian Leary a.k.a. her tenth-grade boyfriend before he decided that he loved God more than girls.

Wow, this is awkward, Alyssa thought.

"Hi, Alyssa," he said. "I didn't see you at the funeral."

Alyssa debated whether to tell him the truth or not. "So about that," Alyssa said.

But Brian interrupted her. "What's with the Klean Kanteen?" he asked.

"Um, well," she began.

Brian's tone turned harsh. "Maybe you should go."

"Wait, no, listen," she said as she glanced over at the bulletin. According to the weekly listing, the confession times were now. "I'm here for confession."

Brian groaned.

"I feel like that attitude isn't very priestly," she said.

"Fine, come on," he said, as he led her to the confessional.

She got behind the screen and knelt. "Bless me, Father, for I have sinned. It's been seventeen years since my last confession. Okay. What do I do now?"

"Just talk to me, Alyssa."

"Okay," she said, though she wasn't sure where to begin. "About six months ago, my boyfriend died."

"I'm sorry to hear that."

"And ever since then, he's been following me everywhere."

"Alyssa, don't," he said.

"Don't what?"

"Make a mockery of the sacrament. Are we done here?"

"Wait, Brian. Just come with me. Please, I'll show you."

Brian let out a sigh, got up, and said, "Okay, lead the way."

He followed her out to the parking lot, checking his watch, as if he had better things to do like turning water into wine or walking on water or turning palms to ashes. She thought of the ashes nursery rhyme while looking for her corpse ex.

"Look, there," she said triumphantly, pointing to the skeleton across the street, which was standing there waving somewhat happily. "I think we're safe here, Father. I don't think he can come onto the church grounds or whatever."

Brian squinted, looked from the skeleton to her and back to the skeleton again. "Start from the beginning," he said.

"Well, I was trying to."

"You have to admit that this whole scenario is a bit,"

Brian paused as if he was searching for the right word.

"Stressful?" Alyssa suggested.

"I was thinking more along the lines of strange," Brian said. "But I could see how it could be stressful for you. Okay, so tell me what happened."

They continued watching the skeleton, which now appeared to be doing some kind of creepy *Beetlejuice* inspired line dance because, when it shook, body parts fell off. But the damage didn't appear to be permanent because he just put the detached bones back on. He was persistent for a bone man.

"Luke," she said, pointing to the skeleton, "died six months ago, and, honestly, at first, I was a bit relieved because it kept me from having to break up with him. I mean, I know it's a sin, but we lived together. And we had a house together, and untangling our lives just seemed so complicated. In a way, death kind of seemed simpler."

"How did he die?" he asked. "Like you didn't kill him or anything, right?"

Alyssa gave him a look. "Okay, maybe, back when I was young, I used to throw eggs at people's houses for Halloween, but you did, too. And, yes, I was trying to steal holy water, but it was for a good cause. And do you seriously think I've ever killed someone?"

"But how did he die?" Brian asked again. "And then what happened after?"

"I'm not sure why it matters," she said. "Unless you still think I'm like some creepy killer or something."

"Just tell me," he said. She noted with satisfaction that he was no longer dreaming of miracles that he could perform.

"Fine," she said. "He died asleep, alone."

"Cause of death?"

"Brain aneurysm."

"And then what happened?"

"I found him, called an ambulance, and they came and took away his body."

"Did you say goodbye?"

"To his corpse? I don't see why it matters. Is this part of your priestly training or something?"

"No," he admitted. "I just watch a lot of horror movies. And it seems like maybe he has unfinished business with you. So what happened after the ambulance took away the body?"

She sighed. "I called his parents, and they dealt with it."

He asked how long they were together. She told him six years.

"And do you think that calling his parents was the right thing to do?"

"No," she admitted, "Probably not."

Brian sighed. "Okay. I think I know what we need to do."

Brian drove her to the cemetery.

"Have you been here before?" he asked.

She gave him a look. Was this his idea of small talk? "Yeah, I come here every Friday for dates with my dead ex. I bring the popcorn, but he can't eat it, so we mostly just leave it for the birds. What about you, *Father*?"

"Well, I'm a priest, so, yeah, I've been here many times. Have you been here since the funeral?"

"No," she admitted, "I haven't."

"Okay, well we're going to go to his grave, and you're going to talk to him. Sound good?" he asked.

And she said it did though it really didn't. What

sounded good or at least better was not going on a wild chase trying to put her dead boyfriend genie back into a coffin.

Brian parked the car, a Lexus, and Alyssa said, "You know this is kind of a nice car for a priest. Don't you take a vow of poverty or something?"

"Well, that's a common misconception, but no. Priests don't."

"So you can have fancy cars but not pretty girls, got it." She was trying to bait him. He said nothing, which annoyed her even more. "Don't you care that I?" she began.

"I'm just trying to be your friend," he said. "Priests can have friends, and I think you need one."

Alyssa walked left then right, past some smaller gray tombstones. She tried to look like she knew where she was going even though she didn't. She was determined not to admit this, but she felt like he already knew this. In the daytime, the cemetery didn't look creepy. It looked serene, like it wouldn't be bad to spend the rest of your days with the stone and the flower wreaths and the dog poop.

Admittedly the dog poop was more in the minus category than the plus. Alyssa was trying to determine if, when she died, she would want her bones to be placed somewhere like this or if she'd rather have them burned. *Ashes to Ashes.* She wondered if Brian was thinking about the nature of life, death, and mortality, but apparently he wasn't because he asked her, "So what have you been up to lately, Alyssa?"

"Aside from trying to avoid the corpse of my head boyfriend? Well, not much."

"I saw your mom a while back," he said. "She comes to church sometimes."

"Well, that's news to me. I think it's this way," she said, pointing straight ahead. They walked up a steep hill and toward a black gravestone. It was large with curvy writing. The tombstone read: "Luke Warner, beloved son."

"Does that bother you?" he asked of the inscription.

"No," she said quickly. "I mean we weren't married."

"You keep on saying that, but do you think anyone really cares about that kind of technicality anymore?"

"His parents cared. They didn't even ask for my input on the service. And the picture montage they put together had like one picture of us, and not even a picture of us alone. Like we were together in a group with a bunch of other people. His parents keep calling to find out when they can come over and get his stuff. But most of it isn't his stuff, it's our stuff. And they can't have it."

"Do you miss him?"

"I miss not being alone," she said.

"Alyssa, you're not alone," he said.

"If you tell me God is with me, I'm going to puke."

"That's not what I was going to say," he said. "Alyssa, I'm with you."

"You're with me, but you're not *with* me."

"Fair enough. What do you want to tell him?"

"That I'm sorry," she said.

"Anything else?"

"Yeah. I want to know why he never asked me to marry him. Did he not love me? Did he want to leave me? Was he just staying like I was because staying was easier than leaving? Do you think that's good?"

"Do *you* think it is?"

Good wasn't a word she would have used to describe how she was feeling right now. If this was over, then what remained, for her, for him, for any of them?

Brian watched her, then said gently, "He was an important part of your life, and now he's gone. How does that make you feel?"

"You were an important part of my life, and now you're gone."

"I'm not gone in the same way he's gone. You can ask me questions if you want to. Go ahead, ask."

"Why did you break up with me?"

"Alyssa, you broke up with me."

"That's not the way I remember it," she said.

"Because that's not the way you want to remember it," he said softly. "Are there things about him that you also don't want to remember?"

"Yeah," she said, "maybe."

"Come on," he said, motioning to the ground, "let's sit and talk."

"Can we do that?"

"Who's going to stop us? The Ghost of Elvis?"

"Okay," she sighed. "Fine."

"So what things?" he asked.

She sighed. "How far back do you want to go?"

"As far back as you need to."

Alyssa started laughing, then said, "I'll begin my life at the beginning of my life."

"You know, Alyssa. There are other things I could be doing right now."

"Two years ago, I could start there. We had these other friends who had been together as long as we had, but they were married, and they had a kid. And it was like, because they had a kid, their whole life changed. They seemed so anchored, settled. Like they didn't care as much about trivial things like who won what game and which local brewery had a new craft beer, and, while we were there, I looked at Luke, and wondered if we'd ever be like that, tied together in that grounding way, and I didn't think we would, and it made me sad." Alyssa went from sitting to laying in the grass. She felt but ignored a bug crawling up her pants legs. There were worse things. At least the bug was living.

Brian was still sitting with his back against Luke's grave. Absent-mindedly, affectionately, he ran his fingers through her long dark hair as if remembering. "What does it matter though? Once we're gone, we're gone. What's left here, whether it's ashes or bones, they're just remains."

"Brian, do you think you're doing the right thing with your life?"

"Well, I don't know, but I hope at least I'm helping people."

"Hey, give me a hand," she said. He reached over to her, and she felt his hands, solid, strong, fleshy, more than just bones. She wanted to hold onto them, but she knew she had to let them go, and, when she did, she felt the emptiness of air.

"Can I drop you off somewhere?" Brian asked because he had driven.

"I don't know," she said because she didn't want to be alone.

"Maybe," Brian said helpfully, "back to wherever you parked your car? I didn't see it outside the church."

"Oh, yeah," she said. "That'd be fine. It's over by the coffee shop."

As they walked back down the hill to the cemetery parking lot, they watched Luke's corpse fly over to the grave. It was quick, almost like a blur, but it was him, swirling above him then down and down and down and down.

"I think he's really gone now," she said.

He opened the car door for her, and she got in. When he turned the radio on, "Another One Bites the Dust," began to play, and Alyssa burst out laughing.

"Hey," he said seriously, "you okay?"

In response, Alyssa began to sing Air Supply's "All Out of Love—So Lost Without You." To her surprise, he joined in. When she was done, he began to sing Tiffany's version of "I Think We're Alone Now." It was off-key and awful and beautiful all at the same time.

They sang together the whole ride back whatever corny, creepy love/death songs they could think of, including "The Banana Boat Song." When they reached her less nice car on the road outside the coffee shop, she got out and turned to him, ignoring the whir of city traffic buzzing by. "Thank you, Brian. Really, thank you."

"Hey," he said, "No problem. And keep in touch."

"I will. I promise."

"Like you promised me the last dance at the tenth-grade homecoming?"

"No," she said, "this time I really mean it. Also, Joey DeSalvo won't be there, so no worries."

"Ah, how could I forget Joey DeSalvo?" he said. "None of us could compete with his superior . . ."

"Intellect?" she suggested.

"You really do have a selective memory," he said. "Maybe I'll see you in church?"

"Probably not," she admitted. "But I hope I'll see you."

"Aly, take care of yourself, and call, me," he said, "if you need anything. Or maybe just call."

"You know we could kill it at '80s karaoke night at O'Neill's."

"I'll think about it," he said.

Alyssa watched Brian drive away in his swanky car as the light began to fade. She was finally alone, but, as she got in her car and hit the on button, in her head, she could still hear Brian singing Tiffany to make her feel better. She closed her eyes and remembered years ago, how he had gently kissed her to that song, and how eagerly she had kissed him back.

Lift Me Up, Drag Me Down

The near-death experiences you hear about on TV talk shows are the nice ones. The ones with angels and comforting white light and long loved, long missed dead relatives. Maybe throw in a harp or two and a street of gold. They're the kind of experiences you want to write down and go on speaking tours about because they're so encouraging. The message of them all is basically the same: It gets better. You're not alone. Everything has a purpose. God has a plan.

But my experience of dying was nothing like that. When I died, I went to hell. As you can expect, it was not pleasant. I suppose you'll be wanting details. In this age of online everything, everyone wants details, and preferably selfies.

Thankfully, I have no hell selfies, and I wouldn't post them if I did. Social media is mostly us sharing with other people the life we want to have, not the one we actually do. If not a play for my life is the best, we make a play for my life is the worst. *I'm poorer, sadder, more alone than the rest of you saps.*

In hell, you don't get any sympathy, and everyone is too busy enduring the misery of their own pain to compare it to yours.

Which is worse? Death by fire, or death by water? No one cares. They're both pretty horrible, and whatever your hell is, you relive it again and again and again.

My hell was being trapped in the kitchen with Toby that night he pushed me down and laughed and laughed. I was bleeding. He was sorry. Drunk was his excuse. Couldn't he see how crazy I made him? The things I made him do. The broken plates. The bashed-in doors. The cabinets ripped off hinges. Me wanting to say something other than *please just stop* but not knowing what.

They told me they found me on the side of the road amid some grass and weeds and other trash.

Someone left me there.

"You're lucky," they said, "to be alive." Was there anyone they could call?

They looked clean and blessed and purified like they wouldn't understand my hell even if I took them there and walked them through. When it's not your hell, you don't understand how a person is trapped, how that person could ever stay.

I shook my head. "No," I said, "there's no one." But did they have more of that fine banana pudding and a Bible?

They look pleased, and I felt like maybe, if I tried harder, I could have a life filled with church potlucks and women's circles and a Jesus who saved me. I wanted that. If I had an urge to see Toby, all I had to do was go back to hell.

A Tale of Two Cats

The first thing you should know is that all witches aren't *I'll get you my pretty and your little dog too* evil. And we're not all like, *If you kill your friend Duncan, you could be king, so just think about it.*

And the top hat and the broomstick and the striped stockings, those are all very *Hocus Pocus* Halloweeny.

In many ways, witches are just like humans who don't have powers, but they're more attuned to the world around them. Witches can be good, or they can be evil, based on the people and creatures they associate with.

Most people without power have the potential to be powerful. They just don't know how to harness the power inside them or around them.

Witches are like Mario once he finds the squirrels or the mushrooms. They're like humans but supercharged. And once you know that you could be supercharged, why would you settle for being ordinary? Of course, in the words of Spider-Man's Uncle Ben, "With great power comes great responsibility." But sometimes the glamour and glitter of the power blinds you, and you forget the responsibility part.

That's what your friends and your familiar are for, to help you walk the line but not cross it.

Creating storms can be fun, for example. But you have to be careful not to get carried away. Think about the damage to the crops and the livestock.

The damage that we can do without thinking, that's why they burned us.

Sometimes though, your friends and your familiar don't keep you in check like they're supposed to.

Sometimes they do just the opposite.

The worst case that I can think of, the worst case that anyone knows of, though most people who know don't talk about it, is the case of Miranda and her cat, Snowball.

At first, the match between them seemed Heaven sent. They laughed and rainmade and baled hay together and then they danced in the forest. But the forest dancing wasn't innocent, it wasn't like the coven dances that we all did. Instead, it was solitary, secret.

Goody Sexton urged her father to report it to the High Priest, but things had gotten stressful lately between the male leaders and the female followers, and Miranda's father didn't want to make it worse.

He didn't want Miranda to have to stand at the scaffold for all to see, wearing the S for Shame. We didn't know what Miranda had done alone in the forest with Snowball, but we assumed it was nothing good. After that, Miranda looked paler, weaker. When we asked if she was okay, she said, yes, of course she was fine, she was great. And we felt it would be unwise to press any further. We looked over at Snowball, who looked fat and content. He licked his red lips happily while Miranda said that she was just going to go lie down. Snowball purred approvingly. We all had to rest up for tomorrow's full moon.

"Do you feel the wind?" Goody Bradford asked. She was the witch most attuned to the rhythms of nature.

I nodded though I didn't get her point. The wind felt well, windy. And wasn't that what wind was supposed to do, blow?

"Claudia, you, too, could harness the potential of the wind. You have the magic in you. If you just took the time to be still and listen. Here come sit near me by the fire."

Skeptically, I did. "Close your eyes. Take my hand," she commanded. I wanted to laugh. This seemed like the theatrical witch stuff we did for tourists.

"Shh, Claudia. Listen."

I did, and what I heard was piercing, ominous.

"Holy crap," I muttered. Then, I apologized for my outburst. "I didn't think this wind reading stuff was real. What do you think it means?"

"Nothing good," she said. We continued to hold hands as we listened to the leaves rustle. To me, they sounded the torment of the damned. I wanted to shut the noise out, but now that I knew how to communicate with the wind, I couldn't unhear its ominous moaning. I didn't know what was coming, but I knew it was bad.

"Tomorrow," Goody Bradford said, "I'll teach you how to communicate with water."

I wondered what good that would do, but I didn't tell her.

Still, she seemed to sense my thoughts. "Claudia, only the most powerful of witches can communicate with the elements. If I can teach you what you need to know in time, together we might be able to stop this.

The next morning, I woke up late. We all did. On the nights of full moon, we would become creatures of the night. It was colder than it should have been, and, in other times, I might have frozen, but Goody Bradford had covered me in a blanket made from ash and fire. It kept me warm and toasty and sound asleep despite the disturbance of the wind and now the waves.

"Ah, she stirs," Goody Bradford said. "First, we eat. Then, we go to the water."

I nodded. Though I still didn't know what good water

dancing or whatever Goody Bradford had in mind would do us, I was curious. So I followed. Plus, I knew her magic was more powerful than mine.

We stood at the edge of the shore watching the waves break.
"Now," she said, "call them to you."
I protested, "But with the wind, we just listened."
"Claudia, isn't communication a two-way street?"
I nodded but thought *this is crazy*.
"Now," she said, "call the waves."
I did, and to my surprise, they came.

I both longed for and dreaded the rising of the moon. I think we all did. All of us had a sense, though not as great as Goody Bradford's, that everything would come to a head with its rising.
Fair is foul, and foul is fair.
For the ceremony, Genevieve would bang the drum. And Miranda would play the queen. In retrospect, this casting choice seemed unwise. Who had determined that it was a good idea to give a struggling witch such an important role?
At the shore that morning, Goody Bradford had told me, "Every witch has her moment, a moment that determines whether she will rise or fall. When your moment comes, Claudia, what will you do?"

The sky was clear, and the moon was bright, as Genevieve banged on the drum.
The chorus began to say their appointed lines.
"One night in the forest, after the sun had faded, and the light of the moon pierced the darkness, Diana emerged

from the forest."

That was Miranda's cue to appear, but she didn't. Truthfully, I was hoping that maybe she wouldn't come at all.

The chorus repeated the line, and Miranda emerged as if from nowhere wearing a long white dress. With her was her fearsome awful cat, both of their eyes glowing red. *Holy shit*, I thought.

The chorus continued, and, since things were about to go all Stephen King, I wondered if it was really necessary for them to continue saying their lines: "Diana emerged from the forest and showed the world her power."

With that, the forest caught fire, and I knew that the fire was coming from Miranda. Goody Bradford took my hand. I knew that it was time for us to call the water.

"This is going to be hard," she said, "maybe the hardest thing you've ever done. Are you ready?"

What was the alternative, to let all the witches burn?

I nodded.

"Let's begin," she said.

"We call to you, Great Spirit of the Water."

At first, nothing happened, and I watched the fire rage.

"Don't focus on the fire. Call the water."

I closed my eyes and pictured the waves. They began to come to me. And then Miranda's cat stood before me, and I was frightened.

"See the water," Goody Bradford said. I did. I saw it come close, but it stopped just around the cat, as if he was powerful enough to part the waves.

Some of the witches had run away screaming, but a few had stayed to watch. Fewer still came to our aid.

One of them was my mother, who had been dead twelve years. Her voice: "Claudia, calm the wind." And, with the power of my mother running through me, I did.

The leaves, which had been blowing in twisty turny patterns, came to a stop. The fires began to die out.

And, as if by magic, rain began to fall.

Defeated, Miranda's cat disappeared, and Miranda collapsed. The fires died everywhere but around her. They consumed her, and she faded to nothing but a puff of smoke.

Goody Bradford looked at me with pride. I felt like I couldn't take the credit.

"My mother," I began.

"Claudia, that was all you."

A few days later, a black cat appeared and wouldn't leave, though I tried to shoo him. Finally, I fed him mice and birds, and he began to settle in. After the full moon and the fire, we could sleep again at night. I named the cat Midnight, and he nestled by my side, purring loudly. For the moment, at least, everything was fine.

Basically, Don't

Don't touch me. Don't kiss me. Don't ask me where I've been. In the beginning, I told you there were conditions. And you said that they were okay. Minor inconveniences. You'd barely notice them at all. After all, you'd seen worse.

With your ex, the one who told you he'd marry you maybe, if he didn't find someone better. You made a stupid pact.

You said that you'd wised up, realized that there were terms you couldn't live with. You seem to be heading in that direction with me right now.

But what I said to you about wanting to be with you, that was real and true. You said you understood that some nights I had to be outside, doing what we would not speak of. After all, every couple has its secrets.

You said that you wouldn't follow, wouldn't watch, wouldn't stand by the window like a sad modern Penelope waiting for her wayward Odysseus to return.

We are all born broken. Some more than most. You think that you can domesticate me with your garbage new age twelve-step programs. But some urges are primal and ancient. Pre-civilization, there was the wilderness and me, and these urges I have, they won't be denied.

When I'm out there, I'm not the me you know, the one who holds you tenderly and covers you in kisses. I can't tell you more. If you keep asking, keep pushing, you will be the stupid girl in the horror movie who goes out to investigate alone. The forgotten one who never returns.

Stay in the house. Keep the doors locked. Shut the blinds.

Once you see, you can't unsee. And, if we pass the point of no return, everything we've worked so hard to build will crumble. My dear, all marriages are built on illusions. Don't pretend ours is any different.

If I show you more, it will destroy you. But I won't die. I can't die. But I'll miss you and mourn you. Just know that I wanted you to be the last. What happens now is up to you.

You can close your eyes, get under the covers, wait till the wind passes and the light shines. Mornings, you can come to me and hold me. But nights, my darling, you must stay away. Stay inside. Stay safe. Because I'd hate to have to tear you apart.

Searching for the Dead

They say the dead tell no tales, but, of course, that's not true. The dead tell tales, just like everyone else. It's just that most people don't stop to listen. In fact, most people don't know how.

The last day I saw Jonah alive was October 15th. Since then, I've been trying to find him, but I haven't had any luck. I've tried everything. They're starting to tire of my visits to the library. Searches I've done so far: *Summoning the dead, finding your loved ones in the great beyond, how to locate spirits,* etc. But nothing has produced any meaningful results.

Yesterday, the man at the next table, the one with poor lighting, the one I try not to sit at unless all the other tables were full, came up to me, and said: "What's your name?"

"Mallory," I said, thinking he was wanting to make small talk. "What's yours?"

"Mine," he said, 'isn't important. But I have watched you here, day after day, searching furtively, futilely, and yet you try the same tactic again and again. Have you thought about trying something else?"

"Of course, but I don't know what."

"Why don't you leave this place," he said. "Walk around. See if any ideas come to you. Sometimes," he said, "to tackle a problem, you need a change of scenery."

"Okay," I said, but I was hesitant. Though the library was ineffectual and frustrating, at least it was familiar.

But what would I find if I went outside? Maybe, I thought, I would find what I was looking for.

I glanced toward the sliding doors. It felt like I had been coming here for a thousand years. But how long had it been? October 15th was the last day I had seen Jonah alive. But the days since then seemed faded and smudged as if they had been written in ink in the rain and now all the words had run together.

Maybe the nameless man was right. Maybe what I needed was a change of scenery. *But what if,* said a nagging voice in the back of my head. I pushed it down. Flowers. Sunlight. Birds. All of those might help me see more clearly. Jonah might be trapped somewhere. Jonah might be counting on me to save him.

As I walked toward the door, women who seemed unusually pale craned their necks toward me. They looked like scary ostriches. This is what could happen when you spent too much time in the library. I hadn't been out of the library since . . .

October 15th, the last day I had seen Jonah alive, had started out so unremarkably. My 5:45 alarm. The 15-minute snooze. I had my tone set on "I've got you, Babe," as a joke, a reference to *Groundhog Day*, suggesting every morning was the same. In a way, it was. Wake up, go to work. Come home. Eat dinner. Maybe watch TV or make love. Go to sleep. Start all over again. Of course, there were some breaks in the routine but not many. The routine had seemed so rote. We had seemed so stuck in a rut. But, in truth, it was a beautiful rut filled with moments of sheer brilliance and loveliness. A pink sunset. A glowing moon. The orange fire of the sunrise. Jonah's unruly stubble against my face before he got around to shaving. The crackle of bacon. The smell of freshly brewed coffee. The heat from a fire pit in winter. The waves crashing against the shore and the sand beneath my feet on our yearly week-long beach vacation. Pizza cheese dripping off the side of a paper plate. Slurping it up with my mouth. Cold soda popping like morning cereal. Telling a corny joke. The hearty sound of Jonah's laughter. I wanted it back. I wanted it all back.

The librarian at the desk, who vaguely resembled the wiry *Ghostbusters* secretary, said I could not check out.

"But," I said, "I don't even have any books."

"Naw,' she said with a TV show New York accent, "Yew can't check out."

"Wait, what?"

She chewed on super pink bubble gum. "Look. Do I have to spell it out for you? YOU CAN'T LEAVE."

I looked at her with disbelief. "I can't leave the library?" I asked, to make sure I was hearing her right.

"Bingo, you got it, Sherlock," she said.

This was crazy, I thought, so I made a run for it. I felt like the protagonist/criminal in a heist film. I could almost hear the Nina Simone music playing in the background. Door alarms went off. Still, I made it out the door into . . . What was out there?

I woke up and heard voices.

The voices were muffled, as if they were attempting to talk quietly, but they weren't very good at it, I closed my eyes and pretended I was still asleep.

"I told you she couldn't handle it," a woman said to a man. Her snide tone irked me, so I opened my eyes.

"Well, well," said Doubt My Abilities Lady, "Sleeping Beauty awakes."

"Wasn't Snow White, the one who . . ." the man said.

"Let's not argue about fairy tales," said the lady because I thought she didn't want to lose the upper hand.

I understand wanting to quit while you're ahead.

"Maybe just tell her," the lady said. "Rather than stringing her along."

I thought she was going to tell me that Jonah was long gone, long dead, that he was in heaven or hell. Was that the bad news, I wondered, thinking of the musical *Jesus Christ Superstar*, which we had watched in CCD class during Easter Week. Was Jonah *damned for all time*? And, if that was the case, could he maybe have like time off from torture for good behavior? Like maybe it was possible to get a break week where he didn't have to endure punishment?

"Jonah," said the man, who looked like a Dickens novel villain, "isn't dead." Did the man have a black tooth? Did the tooth resemble his black soul?

Sensing my doubt, the woman, who was maybe his wife said, "He isn't lying." She wore a bonnet and had a very Laura Ingalls Wilder kind of vibe. Or maybe she was Mennonite. Was she Mennonite? If Jonah wasn't dead, then what, I thought, was going on?

"October 15th," the woman said, "tell me about that day." What do you remember? I thought about telling her about all my regular nondescript memories. But, instead, I asked about the bonnet. I really couldn't help it. The woman shook her head in annoyance.

"Could I join your religion," I asked, "because mine really isn't sustaining me through this major life crisis?"

"It's not your religion that is the problem," the woman said.

Is this *The Midnight Library*? I wondered. Thinking that maybe they wouldn't be familiar with twenty-first-century literature (based on their anachronistic apparel), I said: "Do I get to choose a book that leads to another life?"

The man sighed. "First, Dante. Now, this."

115

I was guessing that he wasn't a fan of popular literature. "*Beetlejuice?*" I asked feebly.

With irritation, he said, "DOES IT LOOK LIKE YOU ARE IN THE HOUSE WHERE YOU DIED?"

"No," I said, making a mental note not to make any more references to popular films or books. "Okay, I'll bite. Where am I?"

"Hell is empty, and all the devils are here," he muttered.

"So, what, Shakespeare is okay, but NOT the *Inferno?*"

"Shakespeare is kind of like the Bible, he said, though I couldn't help thinking that this was pretty blasphemous."

"So where am I?" I asked again because he hadn't answered the question that he had told me to ask.

"Maybe the better question is where are you not?" he said, maddeningly continuing to suggest other questions instead of answering the ones I had asked. Perhaps I just needed to answer the questions myself.

"I am not at home. I am not in an actual library," I said.

"Okay, you're getting there. What else?" he said.

"I am not living," I said, "and Jonah is not dead." I couldn't help thinking that this was all very *Sixth Sense*, but I kept the reference to myself. Apparently, if it wasn't Shakespeare, it didn't matter. Could I reference Eliot though? Was Eliot considered to be good enough to be referenced by the dead? I got off track wondering while the man continued staring at me.

"Is there anything else you want to ask?" he said.

"Of course, there are other things I want to ask, but what's the point of asking, if you just answer questions with more questions?"

"Ask," he commanded.

"Fine," I said. "What's Jonah doing now?"

The man produced a crystal ball-like device, which I suspected wasn't a crystal ball, and showed me a moving image of Jonah. It was all very Harry Potter, I thought, but I didn't share. But Harry Potter was basically the equivalent of Shakespeare, I thought. It was ubiquitous. Even though I didn't mention it, I suspected that even the dead were familiar with Hogwarts and butterbeer. In the moving image, Jonah wasn't crying. He was with a woman, and he was laughing.

"Wait," I said, "how long have I been dead?" Come to think of it, there were no clocks or calendars anywhere. All I knew that October 15th was the last day I had seen Jonah alive.

"Six months," he said.

Six months! I had only been dead six months, and my soulmate had already found a new girl? Priscilla never did Elvis wrong like that, I thought. Even though he cheated on her. I felt like last year's cheap special edition Starbucks holiday cup. To think I had spent six months searching fruitlessly for Jonah, and he and his Ann-Margaret were blissfully living their best life. I tortuously continued watching Jonah in the moving picture because what else did I have to do? I saw a dog jump up onto pseudo–Ann Margaret's lap and lick her. I'd had enough. 'Can you put that thing away?" I said.

"You sure?" the man asked.

"Yes," I snapped. "I'm sure. Is this hell?"

"You're the Catholic," he responded.

This, I realized, was purgatory. I remembered the prayers. But didn't people have to pray for the souls in purgatory for them to get out? Who, I wondered, would pray for me? Not that scoundrel of a fake soulmate Jonah,

I thought.

"What would you have him do?" the man asked. It was a good question, I thought, and one that I didn't have an answer to. Though a little Biblical, sackcloth and ashes would have been nice. Or a shrine with a candle, like those glass jar ones that they lit for special intentions at church.

"Be more miserable," I said.

"I thought that you didn't want him to be miserable," he said.

"That was before," I said, "when I thought I was dead."

"So," he clarified, "you want the living to be miserable, and the dead to be happy?"

"Life," I said, "is supposed to be miserable."

"Is it?" he asked. "Was your life miserable?"

I thought about it. I pictured Jonah and I walking, holding hands, kissing each other in the rain like in a Nicholas Sparks movie. Jonah and I meeting each other for coffee in the middle of the day because we could. Jonah and I hiking a particularly difficult but satisfying trail. No, I realized, I hadn't been miserable. And I didn't want him to be miserable. Okay, maybe just a little miserable. Or maybe I wanted him to be happy. I sighed. Being the bigger person was hard, especially when you weren't really even a person anymore.

"I'm ready," I said, "to begin my celestial journey."

"The only thing stopping you is you," he said. His female counterpart, who in the last few minutes had come to resemble an unattractive Disney movie witch, had faded away. The man started looking less Dickensian and more George Burns.

"So where do I go now?" I said.

"Wherever you want," he said. "Except not, he

clarified, another life that you pick from a book on the shelf."

"Okay," I said, "I get it."

I walked toward the entrance of the library. No one stopped me. Once I stepped outside, I was in an alley that looked vaguely British and villagey. I passed some wizards. I laughed. I was in *Harry Potter*, I realized. Maybe I couldn't choose any life that I wanted. The one I'd had had been pretty darn good. But I could choose any death I wanted. And mine would include butterbeer and broomsticks. There were worse places to be dead, I thought. Maybe in another fifty years Jonah would join me. Or maybe, I thought, he would barely remember me at all.

The Cold Zone

The car was stuck in the snow, but the sun in the distance kept us from succumbing to the cold, before the sun set, *and it would set*. Temperatures during the day were chilly but bearable, but temperatures at night were a different story.

At each checkpoint, there were pictures of the dead so those who remained could find out if their loved ones were among them. Sometimes wondering about the worst possibilities is worse than knowing them. They tried to remove the bodies. But they could only clean up so much, and those who died after dark were left to freeze. It sounds cruel, but the ice was slow to melt.

I didn't know if we could make it to the next checkpoint, especially not with Tara's bum leg, but the alternative was unthinkable. If we stopped, we wouldn't survive the night. It was not just the cold but the creatures of the cold that came out at night, the only vile things that could survive those temperatures.

Before, we thought that no living thing could brave such cold, but then we found out just how mistaken we had been. I wasn't sure if those things were really alive in the way that you and I are alive. There was something wrong about them, maybe even something evil. We thought at least that only evil could subsist in the cold, that those temperatures were not for the living. But we weren't sure if they were living. Sometimes we weren't sure if we were.

We're not sure how or when global warming became global cooling. It was like the balance of the world became upset, and nature wanted us to pay. Maybe those things were nature itself lashing out at us demanding recompense.

What had we done? We had done everything wrong. We had destroyed the earth.

We deserved this fate, but yet we rebelled against it. The will to survive was strong. Stronger than we had realized. The hardest thing was seeing people dying and leaving them. If you stayed with them once they no longer had a chance, the creatures would get you too.

Now it was just me and Tara. Once we had been a party of five, as if we had been waiting for a seat at a fancy restaurant. As if fancy restaurants still existed. Now they were the stuff of dreams and memory.

Tim gave up hope. He asked me: *Do you think there's a heaven? Do you think they have pie there? Do you think that death is any worse than this?*

It was a question that was answerless as long as we were living. Was anything worse than this?

Out of fear of rebellion, the government had to do something. So they established the safe zones, the checkpoints. If you could make it to the next one, you could survive. But you couldn't stay, you had to keep going. If you could make it to the last one, you could make it out. Only we didn't know if anyone ever made it out. There were rumors, of course, but some rumors are nothing more than repeated lies.

They used to tell us when the temperatures were going to drop below zero. Now they didn't even bother. The emergency radios only reported when something was truly different or new. Below zero was nothing new.

Tim's death though, that was something new. They said he was a hero. He had died killing a monster. There were many others still. But, in death, he had saved the rest of us. If I was honest, I wasn't sure if I was willing to make that kind of sacrifice. Even for the promise of eternity.

Even for the promise of pie.

Tara asked me the question that was on both our minds: "What if we don't get the car out?"

I wanted to tell her the truth. "If we didn't get the car out, then we are dead."

But instead I said: "If we don't get the car out, then we walk."

Tara was shoveling frantically around the left wheel, while I manned the right.

"This might be enough," she said. "Get in the car and try to drive through. If it's not, I'll shovel some more."

I looked at my watch: 16:15. Sunset was fast approaching.

What was it about death that so many people linked it to darkness?

I got in the car and pressed the gas pedal, but there was nothing but spinning wheels.

Tara was sweating in the cold. I saw the droplets run down her face.

I thought about suggesting that we just stay here, huddle up in the car and take our chances. But that look of determination.

"You shovel, I drive," she said.

We traded places, and I pushed against death.

Finally, we broke through, and I got back into the car. She pressed the pedal to the floor so we could race to the checkpoint where we would find gas and food and temporary light. We might die, and it might be soon. But life held out her hand to us once again, and we grabbed on as hard as we could. We weren't ready for death, at least not yet.

Mirror, Mirror

There are times when I wake up and look in the mirror, and I don't like what I see. There are other times I don't see anything, and that's what scares me more.

I asked my mother about this once, and she tried to brush it aside as she does with the black bugs that sometimes land on her hair. Maybe it was the angle, she said, or maybe the light was bad.

But that explanation made no sense. Then, I let it go, but I know that she knows more than she's saying. I debated what to do. I didn't want to be thought of as the town freak, the girl with no reflection. I tried to figure out plausible explanations. Was I a ghost? A vampire? Why was it that my image could sometimes be seen but not always? Did I have only part of a soul?

My family was mostly preoccupied with my Uncle Frederik whose teeth had run off again. We suspected that they were with his ex, Helena, because they didn't agree with his decision to call off the wedding.

I thought I might try asking my sister, Theodosia, indirectly, if she had ever seen anything in the mirror that displeased her, and she gave a little laugh. I should have known better than to ask her because she was pretty and vain. "No, of course not," she said. "I always look beautiful." With that, my sister slunk off in a long pink dress and went to go admire herself in the gold-rimmed, full-length mirror in the bedroom. She spun and spun as she admired her long blonde hair and milky skin dabbed with just the right amount of rouge to add color. When I wore makeup, it was to add light. I didn't dare to stand beside her, fearing that my reflection would appear dark and bleak next to her natural sunshine, if it appeared at all. Instead, I stood there lurking in the hallway wondering what it would feel like to look at yourself and not be surprised, even horrified, by what you saw.

Realizing that I might not be able to find the answers I sought at home where the truth seemed to be hidden and obscured by the light of day and the beauty of flowers, I decided to go seek answers in the less polluted, purer air of the cave. But, before I did, I grabbed my phone. I needed to know if Uncle Frederik's teeth and/or his ex came back home while I was gone. Before leaving, I checked my GhoulBook notifications. The ads were the usual. *Do you want to appear less dead? Tips for successfully robbing a grave without being caught.* And, of course, *Flesh Eating 101*. Most of us had mastered that long ago.

I know what you're thinking. Why would a ghoul be able to see herself in a mirror? But ghouls aren't vampires or ghosts. Ghouls both prey on and have souls. We're less romanticized than our undead spirit cousins, the vampire. No one wants to have their face sucked on by a ghoul. But, when you think about it, is having your blood sucked out of your body really that much better or better at all? Though we don't get much credit, think of how much more rotting flesh there would be if it wasn't for us. We are like the waste removers of the universe. And, usually, those we dispose of have long deserved to be removed from the earth even before death. To keep a low profile, the ghouls in my family wait for the evil to die before we prey upon them. The souls we feed on deserve no rest. So, in a way, we exist to carry out justice.

I gathered up the necessary supplies—a helmet, a climbing harness, gloves, coffee beans, and a bottle of water—and left a quick rune by the door explaining my whereabouts. Then I headed out toward the cave. The air outside was damp and fog filled, which I took to be a good omen. I walked and walked till I heard the cries of the damned. Then I knew I was headed in the right direction. I continued walking through the forest of forgetfulness into the cave of memory. I knew I was where I needed to be when I saw the fresh corpses. Ah, I thought the sacrifices. I planned to try a different tack and seek to gain admission to the cave with a different kind of offering. In my pack, I had a jar of light. Trolls would die if they stepped out in sunlight, but they could tolerate it contained. Not only did the light jars fascinate them because of their forbidden beauty, but the trolls could also use them to fend off vampires, who could not stand even small amounts of light.

"Who goes there?" the cave troll asked.

"It is I, Eimi, daughter of Lyra and Niko. I come bearing a light jar and fresh prawn. In exchange for this offering, I seek answers."

"You may enter," the troll said.

I was not afraid. Though trolls had been known to eat anything and everything, including stones and humans, they were no match for huntress ghouls like me.

I put my offering down, bowed, and waited. If my offering was acceptable, I would be granted answers. The troll ate my delicious prawns and stared and stared at the light. If the troll did not accept my offering, I would take the light jar back and return to the village. I cleared my throat.

"Eimi," said the troll, "what is it that you seek?"

I sighed. "I want to know why I sometimes don't see myself in the mirror and my sister always sees herself."

"Come," the troll said, "with me into the cave."

I followed down winding walkways past stalactites and stalagmites until we reached a small reflecting pool.

I hesitated because I was afraid. I closed my eyes, took a breath, then I looked. I gasped at what I saw.

"I'm," I said.

"Yes," he said.

"Half human. Why don't I see this when I look in the mirror?"

"Do mirrors always reflect reality?" the troll asked.

"No," I replied, thinking of fun house mirrors. "Sometimes they distort it."

"So what do you think mirrors created by ghouls would show?"

"What ghouls want you to see," I said.

"And your sister, what do you think she looks like when she isn't presenting herself to look more like a human?"

I thought of what a ghoul looked like when feeding. It was fearsome, ugly. But it was necessary for the work we did.

"And, my mother," I said. "She knows?"

"Of course, she knows. And she is doing her best to protect you."

"From what?"

"From the other ghouls," he said. "Because you are stronger and more powerful than they will ever be."

I thanked the troll and found my own way back to the entrance. While in the cave, I had lost cell phone reception. So, when I emerged, my notifications blew up. The teeth were back. But they had given Uncle Frederik notice that they were staying only if Helena could. So Uncle Frederik welcomed both his teeth and his former, now present, girlfriend back into his bedroom. They resumed planning for the wedding, which, of course, would be on Halloween at midnight in the cemetery. We would celebrate by feasting on bodies and drinking goblets of blood wine. We would be joined by the spiders and snakes.

I noticed, too, that my GhoulBook notifications had changed. Now, there were ads for hybrid ghoul human dating sites and support groups. *Feeling alone*, they said, *we can help*. There was even an ad for a mirror, which claimed it would accurately reflect reality. After all of that, I remained skeptical. Sometimes, we only see what we want to see or what others want us to see. Reality itself is too complex and complicated to be contained in a piece of glass. It's like if you tried to capture the world in a light jar. You can attempt to, but what you get is only a slice of the wider whole.

How It Happened

The dogs wouldn't stop barking. That was the last thing.

They said they had never seen anything like it, how she chopped his body into bite-size pieces. The time it took and all that sawing through the bone.

What they didn't know, what they couldn't, was that this ending was inevitable. Fated. As sure as what the witches had prophesied.

Who could resist that Tom Cruise smile and that good ole boy charm?

Chemistry is a tricky thing, and she felt it the moment she saw him at the tractor pull. This is a mistake, she thought. But some wildfires once ignited can never be contained. And some love stories don't have happy endings.

Was it ever love, she wondered, or just bodies meeting bodies real and raw in sweat and dirt? Is anything ever more than that? Is anything less?

The crows were the first to arrive. And they saw him for what he had become. A crime scene investigation cliché. *DNA evidence shows.* He was the kind of guy everyone wanted to have a beer with. Nobody knew what he wanted in the darkness where she saw him for what he was. Volatile and broken.

The bottle from that last night at the Western bar cutting into her skin. *Some like it rough,* he said.

She thought about her mother and her father, that worthless no-good son of a bitch. Trailer park Archie Bunker. Her mother never left.

There are moments of no return. Chain reactions set in motion that can't be undone. *The defendant feels no remorse.*

If anything, she felt intoxicated. Drunk on pleasure pain.

Whatever possessed you to do this? No criminal record, not even a speeding ticket, and now you're facing 25 to life. After the deed was done and done and done, pieces beget pieces. It all felt so Biblical and true.

Afterward, she didn't bother to wash up or walk away. She felt perfect. With the saw, she had slashed away his sins. She fell asleep and awakened to the cry of morning birds. And then the handcuffs and the chains. But, if anything, she felt free and finally safe.

The Fortune Teller

I decided to start telling cheery fortunes rather than truthful ones because when I made the future seem merry and bright, I got better tips.

I didn't lie, exactly, but I also didn't tell the whole truth and nothing but the truth. When I saw a man whose fate it was to drown in the ocean, I said he would have adventures on the seas. Another pretty brown-haired girl, I realized, would be the sole survivor of a bloody massacre. To her, I said, "You will lose pieces of your heart, but your body will remain whole, and your spirit will be true." She was destined to become an influential gun rights advocate. Sadly she wouldn't see many of the reforms she pressed for passed in her lifetime. But, later, when the important man's son died, it would be her words they would use to fight for justice. Sometimes, knowing the truth does not set you free. Instead it binds you to it like a dog to a chain. You can pull and pull, but being tethered, you can only go so far. It holds you back.

Jeri, the woman who owns the bar below me, says I'm just making excuses. But who is she kidding? People go to her place to drown their sorrows in whiskey, and then they come to mine, pay me my $25 or $50 bucks plus tip depending on how detailed of a fortune they want and how much they like what I say.

I've learned to get good at doling out small riddles that both contain and obscure darker truths. "You will see great things," I tell one woman, a climber, who is destined to fall to her death. She would see great things, but it's the angle that she'll see them from that I leave out.

Most of the time, it works for me, this "tell them what

they want to hear and get a few bucks in return" philosophy, but some customers are more challenging because when all you see is violent storms, it's hard to conjure beautiful rainbows.

Take Bert, whose wife died young, whose daughter died in childhood, whose only son died a young man. He had one grandson, but he, too, was destined to die (in his 50s) of prostate cancer. Bert came to me at age ninety-three wanting to know his future. I sensed that it wouldn't be a comfort for me to tell him that he would live two more years. Mostly everyone he'd ever cared about was dead, and some for a very long time. So, I said, "You'll be at peace soon." He seemed satisfied with this and slipped me a $20.

Jeri, who sometimes came up to watch me do my thing during her breaks, asked me after, "Do you ever get tired of telling lies?"

She said this once the client left, while she poured me a fireball and watched me drink. I liked watching her work because alcohol didn't lie. It either was, or it wasn't, good. When it came to alcohol, there was no hedging your bets.

"Well?" she said, while resting her chin on her hands, her sea blue eyes unnervingly drinking in my face.

"You know it's good," I said. Whatever she had added to the whiskey both enhanced and complimented its flavor. It was sweet and hot and perfect, just like Jeri.

Jeri got up off the stool and moved toward the stairs. I watched her walk away. She wore black leather pants so tight that with each movement you wondered if they would rip. But they didn't. They highlighted her hourglass figure and left nothing to the imagination.

"If I see any customers who need you to blow smoke up their ass, I'll send them your way," she said.

"I'm sure," I said. Though she teased me, I think she

liked watching me work, too, because what I did was so different from what she did. What I did was abstract. What she did was concrete.

Jeri gave them whiskey or vodka or gin to make the forget their troubles. I gave them words to buoy their spirits. And half-truths, unlike alcohol, didn't kill people. Or they didn't usually. My fortunes weren't going to change people's fates.

Except maybe in the case of Adam. Adam was one who came in with loads of negative energy. Sometimes, when people walk into a bar or a fortune teller's shop above a bar, you get a vibe off of them. Adam's vibe screamed *run*, and I'd begun to wonder if I should have.

Instead, I turned on my brightest for-customers-only smile and watched him walk through the doorway into my shop.

"How can I help you?" I said to Adam. He was tall and lanky, dark hair, brown eyes. He looked clean cut.

But the vibe I got from him was very Michael Myers, and I thought there must be some mistake.

What is it that they say about serial killers? That they can seem normal and charming. Well, that was kind of the feeling I got from Adam. I could tell that something was deeply wrong the moment I laid eyes on him.

"I want you to tell me my fortune," he said.

"Sit down," I said. "And put out your hand."

He obeyed. He's not going to kill you, at least not tonight, I told myself. But I wished that there was a way that I could gracefully escape, like I wished there was a curtain I could hide behind or a back door exit I could take. But I couldn't. Because there was only one way in and one way out.

The moment I touched his hand, it was like I had been

shocked. I saw images of women screaming. Young women, old women. Rich women, poor women. And a scared little boy.

Maybe, I thought, I wasn't seeing images of the future but of the past. Sometimes, it was hard to sort out the two.

"I'm sensing trauma," I said.

"Tell me more," he said. I could tell he wasn't going to help me out at all.

The next image I saw was Adam kissing a woman, hard, but it was consensual. I saw other images, but I didn't tell him.

"You're going to take a lover," I said.

"And?" he asked.

"This one's on the house," I said. "You owe me nothing. That's all I can see."

Fridays and Saturdays, Jeri worked late and so did I, but we didn't always get done at exactly the same time because cleaning up a bar was harder than cleaning up a fortune telling studio. My messes were usually psychological while hers were usually physical.

Sometimes I waited for her. That night, I didn't.

That night, I wasn't surprised to find Adam waiting for me.

I knew I would be his lover.

"Where we going?" he asked.

"The Days Inn on Route 11," I said. I wasn't comfortable taking him home.

Back at the hotel, we made love for hours. I wasn't surprised to find that he was gone by morning. He knew where to find me.

When I picked up my phone from the nightstand and checked my notifications, I had a text from Jeri.

I thought you might wait for me last night, she wrote.

I lied to many people, including people who were paying me to tell them the truth. But I wouldn't lie to Jeri.

Something came up, I typed.

Maybe tonight, she said.

Maybe, I wrote, *Let's just wait and see.*

Adam didn't come back that night, and I was relieved. Maybe he wouldn't come back at all. Maybe what I sensed had been wrong. It was rare, but it occasionally did happen. I knew that Jeri wanted me to wait for her after work, so I did. Then I followed her home. We made love on her couch. It was pleasant, tender, familiar. But there were a few times that I thought of Adam, and I felt guilty. I had no reason to. Jeri and I weren't exclusive. She had other lovers, and so did I. But what I was doing or about to do with Adam, I felt like it could consume me. Part of me wanted it to even though I suspected it could be dangerous. For who, I wasn't sure.

Adam returned a week later, again on a Saturday night, and I was glad to see him.

"Back so soon, cowboy?" I said.

"I thought you'd be missing me," he said.

I was, but I wasn't about to tell him that.

"You're awfully sure of yourself," I said.

"This time, I want you to tell me my fortune, no excuses." He threw down a fifty.

After last week, I did feel I owed him the truth.

"Are you sure," I said, "you want to see what I see? It's not always pretty."

"I'm not paying for pretty," he said. "I can get pretty anytime, anywhere. What I want is truth."

"Okay," I said. "Put out your hand."

What I saw, it was hard to watch. "I see women screaming," I said. "At least fifteen different women. And I see a little boy. I don't know what your relationship is to the women or if you are the little boy. When I touch you, I see so much pain."

Adam jumped up from the table as if I'd burned him. He didn't leave a tip. He wasn't waiting for me when I left. I drove to the Days Inn anyway on the off chance he was there. But I didn't see his car. So I drove home, alone. That's what I get, I thought, for telling the truth. But I knew it wasn't over.

What I didn't know is if I would be one of the screaming women or if there was another way this story could end.

The next night after I got done with work, Adam was waiting.

"I want you to get in my car," he said.

"I can't leave my car here," I said. "Someone might think I was kidnapped." Would they be right? Was he trying to kidnap me?

"Are you afraid of me?" he asked.

"Yes and no," I said. "But I'll come with you, if you let me leave my car somewhere else. You just have to trust me."

We decided to take my car to the closest all-night diner. It was crowded that night, and no one would notice if I left it there for hours.

How long, I wondered, would it take someone to notice if I never came back?

I got in his car and fastened my seat belt. I debated whether to ask him where we were going. I worried that a question like that might set him off. I still didn't know what kind of man he really was. I was getting conflicting messages.

We drove in silence for a while. I'm not sure how long, maybe five ten miles. I wasn't keeping a close eye on how far we had gone, though I realized that I should have been. I also should have told someone, maybe Jeri, where I was headed just in case. But I didn't want to think about that. When the silence finally got to be too much, I asked, "So where to?"

He didn't tell me. Instead, he just said, "You'll see when we get there." I didn't know if I should be scared. But I realized that being scared wouldn't change anything. It wouldn't help. And I needed to keep my wits about me in case I had willingly gotten into a car with our local Ted Bundy. I thought maybe if I concentrated hard enough, I could see who or what Adam was. But all I saw was the boy. Who was the boy?

Sometime later, forty-five minutes, maybe an hour, we pulled up to a remote cabin in the woods. I suspected that we wouldn't have any cell service here. So, if he wanted to kill me, he could, and easily, and no one would be the wiser until someone noticed that my car had been sitting too long at the diner or Jeri realized that I was missing.

"I want you to make love to me here," Adam said as he opened the door to a cabin that looked like it hadn't been used in fifteen, twenty years.

He left me to a musty backroom with a mattress in the middle of the floor. There were no sheets.

"On the bed?" I asked. Though I was hoping he had a different plan.

He said no. He pointed to the floor.

When he touched me, I could see the women more vividly. I could see them being thrown against the wall, being dragged by their hair, choked. I saw them being strangled, their necks snapping, and I tried to block out the images. I tried to focus on Adam. Adam, I realized now, was the boy.

Adam didn't make love to me hard. Instead, he made love to me gently, tenderly. I tried not to cry, but it was difficult because all the while he touched me, I kept seeing the women and the boy.

Afterward, Adam took me to his car and drove me back to the city. We didn't speak. Though the drive back seemed long, I was afraid to sleep. I knew that if I closed my eyes, I would see those women and that terrified little boy.

When we got back to my car, I didn't want to get in. I didn't want to go home. I didn't know what I wanted. Maybe just time to process. He pulled into the diner parking lot.

"I'm going to go get something to eat," I said to Adam. "Come with me if you want."

He followed, but I was afraid to touch him. I was scared for what else I might see. So I walked a few steps ahead of him. It seemed very horror movie. The young woman and her creepy stalker.

It was only after we finally ordered, while we were waiting for our early morning breakfast that I asked him, "So how many women did he kill?" Before he could answer, I reached over to touch his hand. What I saw jolted me so bad, that I nearly knocked over my comfort milkshake.

"What?" he asked.

"Why did you take me there?"

"When I thought about that place, I didn't want to see those women anymore, I wanted to see you. I'm sorry. That was selfish. I should have asked you if it was okay."

"You should have," I said. I wasn't ready to tell him what I had just seen, so I didn't say anything. Instead, I excused myself to the bathroom and texted Jeri.

I'm going to have a baby, I wrote.

She typed back quickly, *I take it I'm not the father.*

I wish, I wrote.

Do you? she typed.

Would you settle for being a godmother? I asked.

I'll think about it, she said. *Tomorrow night?*

I didn't know how to respond. *Can I think about that too?*

By the time I got back to the table, our food was there, but Adam hadn't touched his blueberry pancakes. He was graciously waiting for me.

"You sure you're okay?" he asked.

"You're going to have a son," I blurted. Adam put down his silverware.

He eyed me with suspicion. "Any idea who the mother is?"

"Can we just eat our food?"

He reached for my hand, and I saw myself, pregnant, making loving to him. Tears started rolling down my face.

"Do I even want to know?" he said.

"Eat your pancakes," I said, "before they get cold."

I bit into my omelet and tried to focus on the present. The ham was tasty, salty but not too salty, and the man across from me was troubled but handsome, promising. He wasn't a serial killer, and I felt hopeful that he could be a good father or at least an adequate one, and that was better than what most people had.

"I like this," he said as he tore into his pancakes.

"I like this too," I said, looking at him. "Though I had my doubts at first."

Adam reached across the table to kiss me, and I kept my eyes open. I wanted to focus on what was right in front of me. The past was over, and the future would happen the way it was going to anyway regardless of what I saw. For once, I thought, it might just be better to let it unfold.

Under the Knife

Kate woke up excited to see her new face. She had been looking forward to this procedure for months. According to the flashy brochure with beautiful *after* pictures that she had devoured, "the facelifts of today" were different and more natural looking than the facelifts of the past. Kate's need for this enhancement had gone, in the last two years, from want to need. She had all the telltale signs of an aging woman: sagging skin, deep lines, and the dreaded double chin. But recently these once barely perceptible flaws had gotten worse, to the point that Kate could barely stand her own face. Now, when Kate looked in the mirror, she saw a figure that she no longer recognized. A witch. A hag. A crone. A forgettable background character.

She still thought of herself as she had been in her twenties: young, pretty, desirable, the kind of woman that both men and women stopped to gaze at and admire. Things had changed for Kate when she reached middle age. The gray hairs, she could cover up with dye. But there was only so much that modern makeup could do for the skin although that, like everything else, had gotten both more effective and more expensive. She had seven different kinds of anti-aging creams on her nightstand, and none of them had made her look as she had in her twenties: radiant, sultry, youthful.

As for the feeling, her face felt bruised, but this was to be expected, according to what she had read. And she had read so much. Online. In print. Whatever she could get her hands on. *New face, new you,* the brochures had read. Kate was ready.

Kate waited impatiently for the young peppy nurse to

remove her bandage.

"Oh my," said the nurse, as she lifted the gauze. "This is quite impressive."

Kate practically grabbed the handheld mirror. When she saw her face, she nearly dropped it.

She knew to expect bruising, but this. Was this some kind of joke? "Is this?" Kate began.

The nurse pulled out Kate's chart and read Kate her own damning words. "You said that you wanted to look memorable."

"But I don't look memorable. I look terrifying. My face looks monstrous, like something out of a nightmare," Kate said.

"Aren't nightmares memorable?" The nurse asked as she handed her a plastic hospital bag containing all her belongings. The nurse no longer seemed nurturing or young. She seemed like an evil villain from a black and white film, the veneer of her sweetness fading. Kate didn't know what to do.

"You'd best be going now," the nurse said. Her voice had a terrible edge. Kate quickly changed out of the thin gown into her innocuous middle-aged women casual clothes and walked down the hallway toward the front door. When she entered, everything in this hospital had looked so bright and beautiful. But now everything seemed to be tinted with a terrible green-gray color, as if it was rotting.

Katie felt it best to exit and exit quickly. When she turned back to look back at the entrance, which had only a day ago had seemed so fancy and new, the building looked vacant and crumbling, as if it had long been abandoned. Kate was afraid to pull out the pocket mirror from her purse. Instead, she walked into the diner across the street.

I wouldn't mind a piece of pie, she thought as she looked for a server. But, once inside the diner, she saw that here too the welcoming facade was an illusion. This wasn't a diner but a hall of mirrors. And, on every surface, Kate saw her own magnified face: old and scarred and imperfect. Kate took a breath. Then, she let out a long slow scream.

The Fixer

Administering CPR to a robot was a different skill set, and not every technician could master it. So those who could do it and do it well were in high demand.

Frank Zimmerman was one of the most sought-after robot technicians in the city. In fact, Frank was so good that when he was on robot watch, he could demand premium pay. Because, in his fifteen years of doing this, he had only lost two. One of them was a freak, a fluke, a robot who had total system failure. The other one was Vanessa, his wife.

He had gone over her death so many times. He had examined every possible cause in depth except the one he was unwilling to accept. Maybe, he thought, he had been sabotaged. But not by Vanessa, not his Vanny, the love and light of his life. Someone had cut the cord to the robot defibrillator, effectively derailing his efforts to resuscitate her, and he hadn't known until it was too late. Because he refused to believe that Vanny would ever do that. Not just for his sake, but for the sake of Noah, their half robot, half human son, who was curious, precocious, delightful. Even at the age of two, the age he had been when Vanessa died, Noah was a wonderful child. Even if she and Frank sometimes had their differences, he knew that she loved him with a smoldering intensity, and she had definitely loved their son. He knew that without a doubt.

But it was because of Vanessa's death that he had become the skilled technician that he was today. Still, he would give it all up, all the money and the fame and the prestige to have Vanessa back.

Because he was Frank Zimmerman, the best robot

resuscitator there ever was, everyone knew him, and they would have known him even without his black polo shirt emblazoned with the word *Security*.

Tonight, he was working at a high-profile event at the McIlvaine Estate, and he knew that things could get very, very crazy, very quickly. There would be alcohol. There would be drugs. And there would be juice. For robots, juice was the most dangerous of the three. A few milliliters change in dosage could mean the difference between a pleasant buzz and a quick but tortuously painful death. But the skilled technician knew how to spot the signs of impeding death in time to prevent it.

After Vanessa, Frank had put in place certain precautions to prevent a repeat performance of his greatest personal and professional failure.

For every event, no matter how large or small, he always made sure had at least two technicians working with him, one human and one robot.

This was for a number of reasons, one being that humans and robots saw things differently. What one missed, the other might catch. To this day, Frank wondered if, had a robot been with him that night, he might have able to save Vanessa.

"Sometimes though, when it's someone's time to die, it's their time to die," Felicia, his most trusted robot assistant, had told him. He didn't agree with her though. Technically, as long as you maintained all their parts, robots could live forever. Unlike humans, they didn't have to die.

Because Felicia was the best, second only to Frank, he had her working tonight. This event was important, so he had a staff of seven: three robots, three humans, and an alternate in case anything happened to one of the members of his core team. Usually, his team was in top shape. They ran daily. They went to the gym. They completed drills. One of the requirements of working for Frank Zimmerman's team was that you had to be in peak physical health. He had seen things go wrong when the technicians you had on duty were physically or mentally impaired. So Frank did random temperature and drug checks, biannual vision tests, blood pressure checks, and EKGs. His employees could wear contacts or glasses or take medications. He just needed to know that, with correction, his employees could perform. They were like the Olympic athletes of their field, and they needed to be quicker, smarter, and stronger than both their competitors and those who would attempt to outmaneuver them. Their competitors were many. Most were cheaper, but none were better. When a potential client wanted Frank to come down in price in line with many of the others, all Frank had to do was pull out his fancy charts. "Let me ask you a question," he would say to the young punk in the suit who mistakenly thought he could out negotiate Frank Zimmerman, "can any of my competitors boast *these* save rates?" Frank Zimmerman's save rate was 99.5 percent, and he knew that his closest competitor's save rate was fifteen percent less. In the end, most potential clients agreed to pay what Frank was asking because robots were valuable. Much more valuable than humans. They could be programmed to do the toughest most intellectually or physically challenging jobs and do them better than humans and for far longer periods of time under much harsher conditions. If there was a shortage of computer engineers, surgeons, or even Hazmat workers, they could turn to the robots. The robots could endure hardships like extreme cold and nuclear radiation at levels that humans couldn't, and they could tackle intellectual challenges without letting their emotions get in the way.

That wasn't to say that robots couldn't feel. Vanessa felt for Frank. He knew it was real because she could have chosen to live alone. Some robots even slept in pods and turned themselves off at night. But Vanessa had chosen to live with him, to stay on, to have a child. Had she not wanted that, all someone needed to do was flip a switch to neutralize the growth inside of her. But Vanessa had been ecstatic when she found out that she was going to have a baby, and Frank had been too. Even though he knew that some men wouldn't have been, that some men just thought of the robots as merely machines or sex toys, that they didn't see them as fully human, Frank knew that the connection one could form with robots was just as real as the connection they formed with any other life form, including humans.

Frank was walking the perimeter of the McIlvaine Estate because working security at robot-human events included all aspects of health and safety, from breaking up robot-human fights to looking for suspicious activity on the grounds. At highbrow events like this, it wasn't uncommon to see gate crashers, robbers, and all kinds of scammers. Even though Frank had a ticketing system that was nearly foolproof—he scanned the chips that were implanted in the guests' necks and matched them to their photos on their government issued IDs—Frank didn't underestimate the importance of good old-fashioned footwork.

Just as Frank was examining the front bushes for potential intruders and spy cams, he got the radio call from Felicia.

"Frank, we need you in Quadrant 2. We have a

potential salamander." For every event his people worked, he divided the property into quadrants. The quadrants were never the same, so that anyone technologically sophisticated enough to hack their secure radio channels still wouldn't know what they were talking about. And the code word salamander had nothing to do with water creatures. It meant that there was potential salt in one of the robots' power lines.

"Roger, Felicia. Administer some frog leg potion and keep me posted until I get there with the magic wand."

Frank was telling Felicia to give the robot a steam treatment until he could get there with the portable robot-sized power washer. Salt in the lines could cause outages, chip malfunctions, and even death. And salt didn't just appear. It had to be placed. In other words, it was quite possible that someone was trying to kill one of the robots. Frank picked up his pace. He didn't want to appear panicked, but he also didn't want a fatality to occur because he was walking there as if he was taking a leisurely stroll in the park.

When Frank got to Felicia's location, which she transmitted to him by GPS, Felicia pointed to the victim. A female robot in her twenties. She was sitting on an ivory lounge chair gasping for not air, because robots didn't breathe, but life. She had long brown hair, olive robot skin, and she reminded him of Vanessa.

"What's her name?" Frank asked.

"Sir," said Felicia, "I don't see why that matters."

Frank was annoyed. "Never mind, I'll find out myself."

"What's your name?" Frank asked as she continued gasping.

"Bri," she began, but started coughing before she

could finish.

"I'm Frank, and everything is going to be okay. Open your mouth, so I can clean out your system. Do you want to stay powered on for this?"

She nodded. Frank got out the tiny power washer and explained to Bri what he was doing. "This," he said, pointing to his wand, "is going to clean out your lines with steam. It's going to be hot, but it won't hurt. Okay?"

She nodded again, and he began the procedure to clean out her system. "You might want to close your eyes and think of something pleasant like skating or baking while I remove the salt from your system," he told her.

The actual process was easy. He used the heated water to break down the salt and clear her out. It was like what you would do with salt encrusted power lines but on a smaller scale because the power lines were inside her.

The day Vanessa died had seemed rather ordinary at first. Frank had gone to work. At the time, he was working construction and doing robot resuscitation as a side gig. When he got home, he, Vanessa, and Noah had Thai takeout, one of her favorites. He had picked it up after work. Noah was babbling happily about lions, which he had recently seen at the zoo, and Frank was asking Vanessa about her day. She was answering his questions, but she seemed oddly distant. She said that she didn't feel well and was going to lie down. He sat on the living room sofa to watch a sports talk show and said that he would put Noah to bed. An hour later, when he went to check on her, she was dead.

Frank asked Bri if she was doing okay. She nodded hesitantly. He told her to stay with him. He took her hand

and told her that she was doing really well. "You might feel a little weird," he said, "as the salt makes its way through your body. But we'll be here, monitoring you. You might feel better if you get some sleep."

She nodded, and Felicia took her to the recharge bay. Through a computer, one of the other technicians would monitor her water, acid, and fluid levels. If anything went wrong, he would be notified immediately.

"Do you think," he asked Felicia, "that someone tried to kill her?"

"I think," she said, "that we need to check the salt levels in her drink and everyone else's."

"Yes, of course," he said. Normally, he would have suggested that. After all, it was in the protocol, which he had written himself. But that girl had gotten him spooked, and he was thinking about Vanessa. Come on, Frank, he said to himself, get your head in the game.

"You and Thad get on that right away," he said. "I'm going to get back to checking the perimeter." But he didn't go back to checking the perimeter, at least not right away. Instead, he went to check on the girl. She was so beautiful, so peaceful, so much like Vanessa. Even though he knew he shouldn't have because the first rule of robot resuscitation was not to get involved with the robots he saved, he took the robot's hand. Asleep, he thought, the resemblance to Vanessa was even more pronounced. The girl stirred, and Frank froze.

Without looking at him, the girl said, "I'm glad you're here, Frank." Frank realized that she had wanted him to be here. Had she planned this? Had she poisoned herself? If so, why?

"I know what you're thinking," the girl said. Frank thought that the girl was going to mention the poison, but instead she said, "I know you think I look like Vanessa. Vanessa was my sister, my sister model, I mean. And so we shared some parts of our consciousness. I know how she died."

Frank felt like he'd been punched. How much of his life had he devoted to finding this answer? And now that he was here with this girl was offering it to him, he wasn't sure that he wanted it. Something like that, so big, had the power to heal him or shatter him completely. Frank handled it by changing the subject. "Do you know what happened to you?"

"Of course," she said, "the ambassador's wife tried to eliminate me because her husband is in love with me. But the irony of it is, when he hears about it, he will know it was her, and he will leave her."

"Do you love the ambassador?"

"I don't think I've ever loved any man, but I know that Vanessa loved you."

Frank felt like he needed a break, a drink. He felt like she was baiting him, and he wasn't sure that he wanted to hear more. He looked over at the sensors monitoring his own vitals, and he realized that they were dangerously close to setting off alarms. He also realized that if anything were to happen along the perimeter that he was supposed to be monitoring, the blame and the responsibility would fall solely on him.

"Look," he said to the girl, "I have to go."

"Frank, wait," she said. But he was walking out the door and into the night air. He could feel his heart pounding. As a precautionary measure, he raised his own alarm levels. The moon was full, and he was feeling anxious. He knew better than to think about Vanessa on a night like this. But because of her robot clone being targeted for murder, he couldn't help it. Because his eyes and mind weren't on the game at a critical moment, Felicia was able to sneak up on him.

"We tested the salt level of all the other robots, and it was fine," she told him.

Frank tried not to react, tried not to show that she had startled him. He had trained for scenarios like this, so he would have fooled most others. But Felicia said, "I know you adjusted your alarm levels, Frank. If anyone else had vitals levels like you have now, you would have sidelined them."

Frank regarded her carefully. She was Vanessa's opposite in every way. She was blonde whereas Vanessa was dark haired, darker skinned, and curvy. Felicia was tall and slim, like a waify super model.

"That girl says she's Vanessa's sister," Frank said.

"Well, she looks like her, but Vanessa's dead, and we really need for you to have your head and feet on the ground tonight. This company of yours, it's not just your life's work. It's all of ours. Here," she said, handing him a vial, "take this."

He looked at her with annoyance. "You know that drugs are against my rules."

"Frank," she said, "you're already breaking your own rules. It's your choice. Do whatever. But . . ."

"But what?" Frank asked.

"Don't fuck this up over Vanessa. How much of your life has she already taken from you?"

Frank thought of his canned response. Vanessa was the love of his life. Vanessa gave his life meaning. If it wasn't for Vanessa, he wouldn't be the man he was today. But he didn't say any of that.

"You know I'm not taking that," he said.

Felicia sighed. "Maybe you should just go talk to the girl and put the mystery of Vanessa behind you." Felicia put a tentative hand on his shoulder. "You know we all care about you. We all believe in you, in this, in your mission, to save the robots. Some of the clients only care about the money. But for you, this is like a calling. You care if we live or die, and you care about that girl, and you would care about that girl whether she looked like Vanessa or not."

"Go back in, Felicia," Frank said. "I'm good here."

"You know, sometimes you don't make our job easy."

An hour later, a younger new employee came out to relieve him of perimeter duty. Frank had people switch places to prevent party fatigue.

The boy's name was Felipe. He had slicked back black hair and the charm of a classic movie star.

"How's it going in there, Felipe?" Frank asked.

"Well, you know the rich, how they sometimes think they're immortal, immune to pain and death? All I gotta say is I'm glad we're working robot rescue duty. The people working human rescue duty have their hands full tonight."

"Plus, it pays better," Frank joked.

Felipe regarded him carefully, as if he wasn't sure if it was okay to laugh at Frank's joke or not.

"Ha, ha," Felipe finally said, "right."

Frank took the long way back into the house, so he could watch the movement of guests and staff and residents in and out the many entrances. From a distance, you couldn't tell which were humans and which were robots. But, up close, there were subtle differences. Robots' eyes didn't dilate in the same way, and their movements were more precise, less jerky, especially when it came to fine motor skills. They were skilled not just at mining and computer work but also at surgery and carpentry. And they were less prone to making errors than humans. Especially when they were off the juice. Frank remembered Vanessa's toxicology reports. There were abnormally low levels of oil in Vanessa's system leading to lubrication failure. But that didn't make sense. It never had. Vanessa was fastidious about doing regular maintenance. And there was no evidence of a leak in her system. Had she not done the maintenance, or had someone somehow drained the oil out? The cut robot defibrillator made him think that sabotage by another human or robot was possible. But what if Vanessa had done that? Frank hesitated before entering the mansion. In some places, humans were passed out on the floor. Some nights, Frank would stop and check their pulses as a courtesy, but tonight he wasn't feeling generous or benevolent toward his fellow humans. They had created the robots to make their lives better, but when the robots succeeded beyond their wildest dreams, they blamed the robots for taking their jobs and their lives' meaning. And, despite all evidence to the contrary, they saw themselves as better than the robots: purer, cleaner, more natural. It was all hypocrisy, Frank thought, because humans were walking around with mechanical legs and pacemakers and artificial bones and had been for a long time. It wasn't, in Frank's opinion, how you came to live on earth that mattered, but what you did when you got there.

To Frank's surprise, when he went to the resuscitation room, Felicia was already there with the girl who was now powered down. He began to ask her what she was doing there, but he already knew. She was there because she knew he would be.

"How's it going in there?" he asked because Felicia was still working the main house but in a different quadrant.

"On the robot end, fine. On the human end, it's kind of a disaster. It almost makes me feel pity for those fools. They are given life so easily and yet all so many of them can do is throw it away. You came here to talk to the girl?"

He nodded.

"Don't bother," she said.

"Felicia, if she knows what happened to Vanessa . . ."

"She doesn't. Frank, what would it do to you if you knew that Vanessa had killed herself because she couldn't bear to be with you any longer?"

"It would devastate me," he admitted.

Felicia gave him a long hard look. He thought he knew what she was going to say next, something hopeful and encouraging. But, instead, she surprised him. "And who do you think would benefit from that, Frank?"

"My competitors," Frank admitted.

"I ran her source code," Felicia said. "She's not Vanessa's sister, but someone built her to look like Vanessa and programmed her to say that. And I wouldn't be surprised if she put salt in her own lines to try to frame the ambassador's wife. She knew she wasn't in any danger. She knew you would save her, and then she could manipulate you." Felicia's eyes flashed with anger.

"It's okay," he said. "It's not your fault."

"But it's robots like her who make me hate my kind."

"Just like all humans aren't the same, neither are all robots. I know you're not like her. I know you care," he said, realizing that she did care, not just about the company but about him, and she had for a long time. "You turned her off?"

She nodded.

"Okay, then," he said, and he leaned over to kiss her.

He watched her carefully. He saw surprise and fear, but not displeasure.

"Frank, we can't," she said.

"Because?" he asked.

"You know why," she said. "because of the rules."

"Felicia," he said, "I made those rules, so I can break them or remake them. Besides, you know we have more people working than we actually need. We always do. And we've trained them well, to the point where I'm not sure they really even need us out here tonight."

"But you insist on being out here anyway so you can save them all in the hopes that one of them will redeem you for failing to save Vanessa. But it never does."

"Um, Felicia, can you lock the door, and can we not talk about Vanessa right now?"

"Fine," she said smiling. After she locked the door, she reached over to adjust his alarms.

"Are you turning them back to normal?" he asked.

"No," she said, "I'm turning them off because if I don't someone might mistakenly think you're having a heart attack."

"Is that so?" he asked.

"Yes," she said, "now let's get this over with, so we can get back to work."

"Yes, ma'am," he said. "And, just so you know, if too much excitement causes a system overload, I know a guy who can save you."

"I think that he already has. I just hope it's not too late for him to save himself."

Hunger

At first, we felt sorry for Joel because he lived where the flowers did not bloom. But then, later on, we envied him. When the famines came, we couldn't keep up with the birds and the flowers and the trees. We could barely keep up with ourselves. June Bradstreet, president of the town council and wife of Marcus, CEO of Parcelton Community Bank, proposed that we should let the flowers die. Seven voted in favor of this plan, three against. Motion passed. The problem was that, when we let the flowers die, the weeds took over, and the bees became angry. Looking for sustenance, and on their way out themselves, they began attacking us. Beestung and demoralized, we eagerly agreed to June's proposal to send a delegation out to The Hallows where Joel lived.

The reason no flowers bloomed out there was because Joel's house was on the edge of a slag pit. It reminded us a little of The Outlands in *The Lion King*. As if to make it creepier, Joel had a guard dog that some thought was a Siberian husky, but I believed he was a straight up wolf. Whatever he was, I was not about to volunteer to join the delegation. Instead Angela Appleton, Ned Struthers, and Giovanni Giuseppe signed up to go. Naively, we sent them off with water bottles and Girl Scout Cookies. When they hadn't returned three days later, the town council pondered what to do. Some wanted to send a search party. Others thought we should sit and wait. The search party proponents won out by a razor thin margin. Angela's daughter, Mirabel, and Ned's son, Tate, volunteered to go. We weren't sure if they volunteered out io concern for their parents' safety or because they were not so secretly dating and a trip to the slag pit, which had once been a hot make-out spot until it was replaced in recent years by the Drive-up at Della's Chicken and Waffles, would allow them to be alone. Three more days passed, and now we were five men down. Outraged, June Bradstreet wanted to take matters into her own hands, but Marcus talked her down from the ledge. "The town needs community leaders like us," he told her. I wasn't sure if I should be horrified or comforted by his remarks. Was he implying that the town didn't need the rest of us? The wheels in June's head started turning. "What if we just don't send anyone?" Angela's husband asked. He had already lost a wife and a daughter. He wasn't willing to also lose his son. "Or what if we send ten men," another proposed. "Why ten?" Ned's wife asked. At this point, she was more curious than alarmed. "Because," said the man chillingly, "if they don't make it back, there's more food for the rest of us." It was determined that ten more people would go. They weren't volunteers. By now, no one wanted to go, so we had to draw straws. I feared for the worst, but I wasn't one of the unlucky ten. But Ned's wife's only other child, a daughter, was. Since we didn't think they would be returning, we held a farewell party for the ten. We did The Electric Slide and The Macarena and sent them off in style. They waved at us stoically as they mounted their camels. We thought if we sent camels then maybe the chosen ones might have a better chance to make it back. Two days later, the camels returned without their riders. Bitter now, Angela's husband suggested that we prepare the camels for slaughter. Ned's wife protested. Ned had been an avid camel enthusiast, and she didn't want to dishonor his memory. Given that the famine was still raging, the carnivores won out. Ned's wife refused to eat the camels. Angela's husband told her to suit herself. A bitter argument ensued. We suspected that it ended hours later in the bedroom. We didn't blame them, they were grieving and hungry. Three months later, the grass began to grow again, the flowers began to bloom again, and the famine ended. We thought we should make one last effort to recover the lost. Angela's husband was now living with Ned's wife, so they didn't join us. When we got to the slag pit, Joel met us. Somehow, during the course of the famine, he had gotten fat. We asked him if he knew about the missing. His response was telling. "You should thank me," he said, "for saving your lives." We didn't press for details. He gave us chickens, and we took them reluctantly. We were afraid to offend him, so we didn't leave them behind. Now that the famine was over, we could afford to be picky again, and most said that they wouldn't eat them. When we got back to Parcelton, we thought about throwing them away. But June Bradstreet, ever a pragmatist, insisted that we let whoever wanted them have them. Ned's wife, pregnant now, took them all and ate them hungrily. We didn't judge her. We hadn't lost what she had lost, so who were we to question how she lived?

Secrets

The blood drinking would not begin till after midnight, which was good because it gave Daphne time to prepare.

They say that your first experience is unforgettable, a gateway to everything else.

Daphne was fourteen, so she was old enough to participate if she wanted to. But she could also choose to wait.

"You don't want to rush it," Serafina had told her.

Serafina was older and a prefect and the only other girl from Daphne's depressed farming town, so, by default, they were best friends.

They weren't dating, as many assumed, though they sometimes held hands in the hallway and had kissed twice. Serafina made it clear that she liked boys, had two boyfriends, maybe three. She strung them all along with false promises of fidelity and loyalty, the kind of promises that men often made to women but never kept. Everyone from Farmington (here that was only Daphne and Serafina) knew that Serafina's father was the town drunk. That was why Serafina had enrolled, to escape the boxed in, cattle feeding, 4H breeding life she would have had. So, when the castle school on the mountain advertised their full scholarship for farm girls, Serafina had jumped at the chance to apply and left for the school the day she got the letter.

Daphne wasn't going to apply, had no interest at all, till the night she woke up to get a glass of water and saw her mom downstairs on the couch so high that she hadn't even seen Daphne walking right in front of her face. Then all her mother's sick days began to make sense. Her father working two jobs to try to keep up with the bank payments while her mother continued her bottom spiral. But maybe her mother couldn't help it. They say addiction is a curse. Ever since that accident with the tractor, she hadn't been the same, squeezing them dry, injecting liquid lightening into black veins. One day, strung out on something, Daphne wouldn't be surprised if her mother dropped a match and burned the barn to bits.

The scholarship for farm girls promised that everything would be paid—room, board, books, even spending money, which Daphne wouldn't spend. Instead, she would hand it over to her father. Though he needed it, he hated taking money from his daughter.

"I've heard rumors," her father said, "about what goes on at that school."

"Don't worry, Daddy," Daphne had lied, "none of them are true."

The girls in her witch history class had taught her well.

"If you excel here," the headmistress had told Daphne, "you could go onto Harvard, Princeton, or Yale. Witches attend all of the Ivies. How else do you think those dumb legacy boys in their secret society gloried frat clubs ever make it through?"

Witches, Daphne had learned, weren't evil. They just did things that most humans would consider to be weird. They didn't kill people, and they didn't drink human blood. No, they drank the blood of vampire bats because it could give them power. Power, Daphne thought, was the opposite of what her mother had, and she wanted it as much as she had ever wanted anything.

Daphne had asked the headmistress one day after sorcery class if witches could cast spells to break the cycle of addiction. She knew the headmistress was wondering if her interest in the matter was academic or merely personal. Daphne's psychic abilities had come to her rather early, and she could read the headmistress' mind.

"Some witches," the mystic had told her during Thursday chapel, "never develop psychic abilities at all."

"Is that so?" Daphne had said nonchalantly, as if she had no interest in the topic at all.

But the mystic saw through her. "Your friend," she told her, "doesn't have your powers."

According to *The Book of Legends*, if a witch who wasn't ready drank from the red chalice, it could drive her mad. "We share the cup," the communion literature said, "because are one." Rumor had it that sometimes witches transferred their abilities to each other by sharing the cup.

In part, Daphne was afraid that, if she drank the blood, it would drive a wedge between her and Serafina.

On the fence about what to do, Daphne considered consulting the Oracle of Flame, which was located just outside the chapel. But instead, she decided to brew herself hot chocolate. Witches had harvested the cacao beans from Ecuador, so their hot chocolate was better than anything Daphne had ever had before. Daphne thought that maybe, if she drank the chocolate, it would lessen her desire for blood. But, while she was melting the chocolate in a cauldron, Daphne had an unsettling encounter with the wood witch. "Put your hand in the fire," the wood witch said. Daphne knew that this wasn't a command she could ignore. So Daphne did as the wood witch asked, expecting the same searing pain she had felt the time she'd accidentally burned herself on the stove. But, instead, Daphne felt nothing. And, when she moved her hand from the fire, there were no scars. Daphne looked at the wood witch with awe. She knew that the mystic had sent the wood witch to persuade her. But Daphne didn't need much persuading. She wanted power, and blood would give her power. If sacrifices had to be made, then they would be made. And maybe, if Daphne drank the blood, nothing would change at all though Daphne knew that was likely untrue.

Daphne was careful not to be the first to show up to the ceremony. She didn't want to seem too eager. But she also didn't want to be last to arrive. She didn't want them to question her commitment to the coven, though Daphne often questioned the commitment herself. Was she here for the right reasons? Most of the ceremony was a blur, but the last few moments, the moments before communion, were clear as the brightest stars.

"If your heart be true, and your motives be pure, please rise to partake of the cup," said the priestess, who was dressed in red vestments because The Night of Initiation was the most sacred night of the church year.

Daphne looked around nervously to see who else would partake. Daphne recognized two girls from her Witches in Literature class and one boy who was the groundskeeper's son. The other members of her class were noticeably missing, and Daphne wondered if she was making a mistake. But all the upperclassmen and of the instructors had seen her in her red veil, the veil of intention, and it was too late for her to change course. Daphne got in the communion line. "The Blood of Our Brothers, the Bats, given for you," the priestess said. And Daphne replied, "Amen." Daphne took a sip and felt the blood run through her. It felt like a quadruple shot of caffeine. After the ceremony, the school hosted a party where the old guard welcomed the new with unsolicited advice and punch and cookies. But Daphne skipped the ceremony and headed straight out into the night air. She knew there might be questions. Some would wonder if the blood had tainted her, if she could handle its power. But Daphne didn't care, and she could not wait to feel the wind against her cheeks. She flew all night, her eyes watering with pleasure, and returned to the school just before dawn. When she landed, the headmistress was waiting.

"Daphne, we should talk," the headmistress said.

Daphne nodded. Why hadn't anyone, she wondered, told her how fabulous this would be? But the headmistress, who was also apparently psychic, read her thoughts. Being around so many psychics could be a drag sometimes.

"Yes, yes, I know that not every witch feels this way," Daphne said impatiently.

The headmistress seemed taken aback. How had she not known that Daphne was a psychic too? And then Daphne realized it was because of the fog she had cast. Sometimes, she could keep certain thoughts hidden from other psychics by casting a fog that distorted and distracted. Now that she knew, the headmistress would try to penetrate that fog. But Daphne held firm. There were some secrets that Daphne intended to keep. So the headmistress resorted to language.

"Who taught you?" the headmistress asked.

Daphne considered lying, but this seemed unwise.

"No one," Daphne admitted.

The headmistress didn't seem to be trying to conceal her thoughts, and Daphne wondered why.

"You don't even realize, do you, that you are breaking through my fog?"

Daphne shook her head.

"Oh, my dear," the headmistress said, "it has been a long time since I have seen a witch with so much power.

Be careful."

In a flash, Daphne revealed some of the things she had kept hidden. "As you can see," Daphne said, "I'm more than capable of keeping secrets."

The headmistress smiled. "You are ready," she said.

"For what?"

"For the real initiation to begin."

I'm Not Karen

Back when we were in college, when most people still had landlines, Sylvia and I had an answering machine that had a glitch. When the machine was disconnected from the power cord, it erased all the messages whether they had been listened to or not.

In a way, it was like the age-old question, if a tree falls in the forest, and there's no one to hear it, does it still make a sound? If a message is left on a voicemail and no one listens, does the message still exist? Or is it just lost in digital space?

It was this question, this fear of not wanting messages to be lost, unlistened to, trapped in mailboxes that compelled me to play all my voicemails. I don't know why it mattered, but I felt that, if I listened, I could set the trapped messages free.

Even if the majority of the messages were useless, telling me that the warranty on a car I didn't own was about to expire, that I had won a lottery I hadn't entered, or that a customer of a plumber with a different phone number needed me to call him back, I still felt compelled to play and release them. I didn't want anything once real to be trapped in limbo, in a state of in-between.

Most of the time, I didn't interact with the callers. I just played the messages and deleted them. But this one message, this one caller rather, was the exception. She called wanting to talk to Karen. At first, I listened and erased those messages too. But the caller kept calling regularly, persistently. So I felt like maybe it was an act of kindness, compassion to call her back and tell her that she had the wrong number, that I wasn't Karen. I didn't know

165

what her name was because the messages didn't tell me. She just said, "Hi, Karen, it's me. Please give me a call."

It was a Wednesday evening after work when I finally did.

"Hello," said the voice on the other end of the phone. I recognized it from all the messages she had left. "Karen, is that you?"

"I'm not Karen," I said. "You keep calling this number, but it's wrong. I don't even know who Karen is."

It was like she hadn't heard me, or she didn't understand. Because she kept talking to me as if I was this Karen.

"Karen, it's so good to talk to you," she said. "It's been so long since I've spoken with you, and it's wonderful to hear your voice." I felt like I had no choice but to listen. Besides, maybe if I let her say what she had to say, then she would stop calling me (as Karen).

Who was Karen to her, and what would she say next? I wondered.

"I haven't talked to you since Georgie died. I know that was hard," she said.

"Yes, it was hard," I said because it seemed like she expected me to say something in response though I couldn't say much because I didn't know who Georgie was.

"Why did you leave him?"

"Who, Georgie?"

"No, Georgie died," she reminded me. "You left Ken after George died."

"I did," I said, agreeing.

"You should come over, Karen," she said.

"I should," I said, "but my schedule's rather busy right now."

"It makes a woman sad when she makes it her life's

work to raise four kids, and none of them ever comes to visit her," she said sadly.

"What about . . ." I began, trying to guess the name of Karen's siblings.

"Oh, the boys," she said. "'You should know by now that most men are useless, except maybe Ken. Ken was a good one, but this is why I'm counting on you, Karen."

"Oh, yes, of course, right," I said. "Listen, maybe I can make some time to visit next Tuesday."

"That would be fabulous," the woman said. "I'll call you Monday to remind you."

This created several problems. One was that I didn't know what Karen looked like and if I resembled her in any way. Another was that I didn't know where this woman lived. The best-case scenario was that the woman would forget that I had said I was coming to see her, that she wouldn't call me Monday to remind me. That she would stop calling me all together. But, of course, that's not what happened.

I knew her number now, and I had even programmed it into my phone as Karen's mom. I didn't answer the first five times she called. But she was relentless. She wasn't giving up.

"Karen," she said.

"Um," I said.

"Why didn't you answer?"

"Because of Georgie," I said trying not to sound uncertain.

"Now, Karen, we've talked about this. You can't use Georgie's death as an excuse to ignore everything and everyone."

"Okay, right," I said. "But, look, the truth is, I'm not

ready to come over to your house. It brings up too many memories of Georgie. So maybe we can meet somewhere else, somewhere less painful." What I really meant was maybe we can meet somewhere public. Maybe if I met her once, she would be satisfied. If not, I could flee, and she wouldn't be any of the wiser of who I really was and where I really lived.

"Karen, why didn't you say this earlier?" said the woman, sounding annoyed, "instead of ignoring me for months and months and months."

"You're right," I said. "I'm sorry."

It was determined that I would meet Karen's mom at the Oak Hill Diner.

"I don't have to tell you where that is," she said.

"Yes," I said. "Right."

I googled the Oak Hill Diner. I didn't think I had ever been there. But the street view pictures made it seem quiet and safe. It was in a nice neighborhood near the college. It looked like a place where I could comfortably eat.

"I'll see you tomorrow," she said. "At six o'clock sharp. And, Karen, don't be late."

I wasn't late. In fact, I arrived 25 minutes early, so I could scope out the place, figure out the best place to park in case a quick getaway was needed. I also wanted to decide what I wanted to order so that I wouldn't waste time staring at the menu while sitting with this unfamiliar woman.

The menu was interesting. From the view I saw of it on my phone, it appeared to be printed on red and white paper that reminded me of an old-time movie theater or a box of Cracker Jacks. It served standard diner fare, but with a twist. Like instead of broccoli cheddar soup, they had broccoli cheddar sandwiches. Instead of mashed potatoes with gravy, they had mashed potatoes with cheese and bacon and french fries with ham and grits. I settled on ordering the mango lemon pancakes just as I heard a tap on my car window. It was a white-haired woman with small square-shaped glasses and a thick winter coat. It was her, it had to be her. But how did she know where to find me or what I looked like? I rolled down my window.

"Karen, what are you waiting for?" she asked. She didn't even seem surprised that I had arrived in work scrubs, my caramel-colored hair pulled back into a tight ponytail.

"I was just looking at the menu on my phone,'" I said.

"Why? You always get the mango lemon pancakes," she said.

"Oh, right," I replied with confusion.

I followed her inside. The diner, like the menu, was red and white, retro. The staff seemed to not only know her but confusingly me. Did I not only resemble her missing daughter but also have her exact same phone number? This didn't seem possible.

"Now, Karen," she said, after we had ordered, "don't be angry, but I have a surprise for you."

"I won't," I said. Because anger wasn't the emotion I was feeling.

"I asked Ken to join us," she said, just as a tall muscular man with a red brown beard walked into the diner to join us. He was attractive, just my type.

I tried to remember who Ken was to Karen. Ken was the man who she had left after Georgie's death, I realized.

Ken approached us. "Karen," he said, "it's good to see you."

"Um, yeah," I said, wishing I could leave before my pancakes arrived, even though I was hungry, having skipped lunch because I'd been stressed about this meeting for most of the day. "Excuse me, I need to go use the restroom."

I got up and walked to the pink door that said Ladies. The bathroom that said Men was blue. Maybe this was to help small children find their way. Children like . . . I needed to orient myself. So once inside the restroom, I called my old roommate, Sylvia.

"Sylvia," I said, "do you know who I am?"

"Of course, I know who you are. We roomed together for two and a half years, including that one awful semester that we lived in that ant-infested dorm that used to be a frat house."

"Okay," I said with relief. "Good."

"Can I ask you something though?" she said.

"Sure," I said.

"Are you still taking the pills?" she asked.

I wanted to ask which pills, but I was afraid I already knew. The pills that made me forget what happened to Georgie. The pills that made me think my name was not Karen. The pills that allowed me to live an entirely different life.

"No," I lied. "I stopped taking them weeks ago."

"Okay, good," she said. "Because Ken was really worried about you, and so was your mom."

"I'm sure," I said. "Look, Sylvia. I've got to go."

I hung up the phone and tried to figure out what to do. On the one hand, there was the woman inside the diner who might be my mother, sitting with Ken, an attractive bearded man who looked like someone I could maybe love or had loved. But I (or Karen?) had left him after their son Georgie died.

"I'm not Karen," I said to myself as I rocked back and forth on the toilet until it became a plea, a cry.

Outside the bathroom, I heard a man who I knew to be Ken banging on the door. "Karen," he said. "Please come out. Please come home."

"Ken," I said with a mix of fear and hope. I started to say, "I'm not Karen" again, but I couldn't, because I knew I was.

The Man I Loved, The Man I Married

I expected John to haunt me, but not like this. The image of his face overwhelmed by water was what I expected to see. But what happened instead? That was next level weird.

The finger writing in the windshield reading "Don't date him," the design of our wedding ring done by Spirograph, the Etch A Sketch drawing of his face. At least I guess he didn't inhabit a creepy doll or turn my dreams into crazy running-away-from-a-monster nightmares. At least there were no zombies trying to tear down my windows. No vampires trying to suck my blood.

Instead, it was odd, intrusive stuff. I was tempted to call him my ghost stalker.

"What is that?" a coworker asked of the Lite Brite image that appeared in my passenger seat. It was a picture of a cake he once baked me.

Oh, that's just John, I started to tell her. But, instead, I said: "Oh that's just something I was going to donate to Goodwill. It was my brother's." My brother had died in combat duty. An honorable thank-you-for-your-service way to go. The way John died, on the other hand. I had so many questions. What was he doing out in that canoe in the first place during that terrible storm?

"My brother," I continued, "really liked cake. I wanted to share the love with children in need."

"But where are the other pegs?" the girl, Jacey, asked.

"Oh, they're in a box in the trunk," I lied. Though the lie was neither believable nor good, she seemed satisfied.

After I dropped Jacey, my carpool buddy, off at her apartment, I stopped by a dumpster and hurled the toy in.

John liked to build art out of playthings. At one point in time, I would have hated to give away the things that reminded me of him. But now I felt all these weird parlor tricks were just going to taint his memory. Did he want me to hate him? Why wouldn't he let me move on?

It was a Tuesday in February when the strangest thing happened: a new car arrived outside our house. It was wrapped up in a bow. The keys were on the mantel. On the driver's seat was a note that read: "You deserve this. Love J." The handwriting was unmistakably his. I wondered, not for the first time, if I was losing my mind. How had this car gotten to my driveway? Was it stolen? Was it paid for? If so, by whom? I didn't think the dealership accepted ghost money. If ghost money did exist, who would be pictured on it? Jacob Marley? I laughed in spite of myself. The situation was so absurd. What was I going to do? Leave it or drive it? I knew John would have wanted me to drive it. But I didn't care what John wanted. John was dead. But part of me wanted to feel what it was like to drive a fancy car like this regardless of whether it was mine. It was a fun thing that I'd wanted but had never gotten to do. Did John know that? Is that why he was doing these strange things? I sat down inside the car and shifted into drive.

John and I met in our sophomore year of college. We shared a love of ramen noodles and walking along the Lakefront. He disliked pizza. And I hated frat parties. Together, we were a pair of college oddballs. We both liked hoisin sauce and swapping care packages. "What'd you get?" he'd ask me when my paper bag wrapped parcel came all the way from Pennsylvania. I'd laugh. "My mom makes

173

weird cookies. I don't know. Maybe Macadamia Mystery?"

John was just supposed to be my college boyfriend, the one I watched Willy Wonka with while he smoked weed. But he became my fiancé and then my husband. At some point, it all became less trippy and fun. And then he died.

I was sad, and I was curious. I was angry about having to go solo to baby showers as my younger, less mature friends settled into marriage and parenthood while I was stuck, stuck with a dead stalker husband.

I took the car onto I-81 and started driving faster than I should have. I found some country station I would normally never listen to and blasted Toby Keith. "How do you like me now?" Keith crooned. I thought about crashing the car into the median. Is that what he wanted? Did he want me dead? Instead, habit and self-preservation took over, and I drove the decked-out car straight to work. When I got done with work, would the car be there? Or would the car be gone, like John?

Sometimes we fought. He said I was superficial. I said he was judgmental.
I remember a car ride home from a dinner party.
"Why," he asked, "did you have to comment on Megan's weight?"
"I didn't comment on it to her. I commented on it to you. Am I not allowed to make an observation? Hasn't she gained weight?"
"Yes," he said. "She has. But why does that matter?"
"What else is there to talk about," I said quietly, "except what we see?"

THE MONSTERS ARE HERE

The day John died was a Thursday, and I was out of town. I felt guilty about that, of course I did. Especially because we had fought before I left.

We had fought about the living room. I said it was too junky. He said it was homey.

"But don't you want to have people over?" I had asked.

"Why, so you can comment on their appearance? If their hair is too messy or their pants too tight?"

"That's not fair," I protested.

"Isn't it?" he asked. I left for my trip the next morning without kissing him. I got a call a day later. He hadn't shown up to work. Did I know where he was? I felt a sinking feeling then, but it was also a feeling of relief. Somehow, I knew it was done. But what I didn't realize was that it also wasn't done. I didn't realize that, even dead, he wouldn't let me go.

I thought of the first weird thing, how it could have been innocent. A fortune cookie in which the fortune read: *Find a friend to eat ramen noodles with.* The friend I was with, a man, said I seemed upset, did I want to go home?

I nodded. I did, but I didn't. When he drove me home and stopped at the doorway, part of me wanted to ask him in.

"Don't date him," said the finger window message that came the next morning. Is this a joke, I wondered, some weird prank played by a neighborhood kid?

The date guy, a nice man my age who liked to wear plaid patterned Scottish scarves, called a few days later to check on me, but I didn't answer the phone or call him back. Maybe it's too soon, I thought. But, in reality, it was the message, written in the frost on my car by the hands of a dead man that deterred me. I had questions. Was it just him that John didn't want me to date or was it anyone? Did John want me to be alone?

When I got done with work, the car was still there in the space where I left it. Inside was a cake. It was round with chocolate frosting. John's favorite. In yellow lettering, the cake said: "Celebrate you." What the hell did that mean? Wouldn't it be better to celebrate me in a normal time, a time where I didn't have to deal with weird messages from my dead husband? Under the cake was a note. The name of a restaurant, one we had talked about going to but never had. "Go," it simply read. I knew the note was from John. I wondered, if I did what he wanted, if he would stop. So I went.

I took a seat at the bar because I had learned over the last few months that the bar was the least weird place for a woman to eat alone. I ordered a Sex on the Beach. When was the last time I'd had sex, I wondered? Had John and I ever had sex on the beach? As I pondered appetizers, I noticed the man next to me. He was handsome, well dressed, and polite to the server. He turned to me. "Are you waiting for your husband?"

I looked down at my ring. "That's a man repellent," my coworker Jacey had once told me. "That's fine," I'd replied then. "I'm not trying to meet men."

"Oh, I'm," I stammered not sure how to explain without revealing too much. "He's not coming."

"His loss," he said. He looked at me with what I thought was desire. I felt a mixture of interest, surprise, and guilt.

"Oh," I said, feeling the need to defend John even though his post-death antics had annoyed and infuriated me. "He would be here if he could. You see we talked about coming to this restaurant. But, well, he died."

"Oh, dear," he said. "I'm so sorry."

"No," I said. "I know he wanted me to come here. And do the things we wanted. The things we never got to do."

"I'm sure," he said.

"Sometimes," I continued, "I don't think we wanted the same things. We fought before he died. And I never got the chance to apologize or ask for forgiveness. Oh, I'm sorry," I said as my pale face flushed red. "You probably didn't want to know all that."

"Bars," he said, "are a good place to talk to strangers. Can I buy you a drink?"

"Oh, I," I hesitated.

"Didn't you say he wanted you to come here?"

"Honestly, sometimes I don't know what he wanted. The way he died was so strange. He died on the river. He went out canoeing in a storm."

"I remember reading about that in the paper," he said. "And being jealous of that man. Jealous of a man who was brave enough to go out canoeing in a storm. The water can be beautiful then. What are you drinking?"

I was embarrassed to tell him, but I did. "I didn't think of him as brave. I mean maybe when we were younger. But . . ."

"My dear, he said, you're not that old. I would imagine you're about my daughter's age. Does that bother you?"

I looked at him more closely. He had wrinkles especially around his eyes, but they looked good on him. His hair was salt and pepper black. He looked old movie star distinguished. "No," I said honestly. "Not at all. My husband, I can't seem to let him go." I felt tears dotting my cheeks.

"Honey," he said, "it's okay." He reached out to place a comforting hand on my leg. But what I felt was interest and need.

"Oh," I said, startled. "I—" I felt my breath quicken. He put his hand in mine. "I don't know you well. But, what I do know, I like."

"It's easy," I said, "to like someone you don't know. Harder once you know them well. John and I, I don't know if we would have stayed together, if he had lived."

"It's hard to know."

"Are you married?"

"No," he said.

"Is she. . ." I began.

"We're divorced," he offered, saving me from asking the hard question. "At first," he said, "that seemed like failure. But sometimes admitting defeat is the wisest thing you can do."

"I feel like we couldn't admit defeat."

"This might seem like a crazy question," he said.

I couldn't help laughing.

"What?" he asked, taken aback.

"It's just that I feel like my dead husband is haunting me, and whatever you have to say probably isn't as crazy as that."

He smiled.

"Have I scared you away"? I asked.

"Just the opposite," he said. "I'm intrigued. A beautiful woman with a mysterious past."

By then, I was nearly done with my second drink. I didn't drink often, so I was more open with him than I otherwise would have been.

"Can I buy you dinner?" he asked. "That was my question."

"Was *or* is?"

"I'm still asking," he said.

"I want to have children."

"Dinner?" he asked again.

"I don't scare you?"

"Just the opposite," he said. "Did your husband want to have children?"

"Sometimes, I think he didn't want to have children with me. He loved me, but I'm not sure he always liked me."

"Hey," he said, "dinner?"

"Are you sure you want to?"

He reached over and kissed me on the forehead.

"Oh," I said. To my surprise and his, I reached out to kiss him back. "I like you," I admitted. "But what if, once you get to know me, you don't like me?"

He looked at me. "I like you. And I suspect I'll like you better once I know you better. So dinner." It was more like a command than a question.

"Yes," I agreed.

"And then?" he asked.

"I want to kiss you again," I said, smiling. "If you let me."

He reached out his hand to me. "Let's go get a table."

I hesitated for a moment then reached for his hand. "I really think my husband is really sending me messages from beyond the grave. And . . ."

"Dinner," he said again. "Okay?"

"Yes," I said, and for the first time in long time I felt like it would be. "Do you want to hear the craziest part?"

He wrapped his fingers into mine. "Sure," he said. "Over dinner."

"Do you think it's possible for a dead man to buy a car?"

"Sweetheart," he said, his hand still in mine, "I still want to buy you dinner."

"And, I want," I said carefully, "to eat in a restaurant with you."

"It's settled then," he said. Nothing seemed settled. Not my questions about my dead husband's mysterious death or the explanations for the hauntings, but, for whatever reason, I had a feeling that things would get better. Maybe I would never know what had happened the day John died or if he loved me in the end. And maybe, nice *living* man waiting to share my company, I didn't care.

Just Like Home

Terrill was not honest with us about the reason that he was sent on the extra planetary ship to earth.

He came to us with that same old same old alien to human "I come in peace" nonsense.

And we, being schmucks, ate it up. We wanted to appear enlightened and accepting. We wanted to think a superior being had traveled light years just to commune with us because we were that special.

It's not like he was a lizard man who wanted to eat us. And he wasn't trying to repopulate the planet or anything with a race of mutant aliens. (In case you were concerned about that.)

Really, it was simpler than that. Governmentally, things had gotten out of hand on his home planet, El. Terrill was a con man, a prisoner, and to prevent crime, his planet's government had adopted a three-strikes-you're-out policy. So third crime, no matter what it was, meant that you went to prison for life.

Well, that was all well and good (okay, it wasn't well or good, but it was better than what came next) until an even more conservative leader had risen to power. There were rising complaints about the costs of keeping a third of the population imprisoned for life. But, rather than addressing those complaints in a humane way (or what's the word if the subjects aren't human—*aliene?*), the new government decided to respond to the complaints by converting all the life sentences to death sentences. They said they would allow the prisoners to appeal, but all the appeals were rejected. Terrill said he didn't think that they were even read.

Terrill was scheduled to die for the crimes of forgery, check fraud, and tax evasion. A prison guard who was sweet on Terrill (he was a charmer) gave him the keys to the escape pod. Terrill said he wished he could help the others, but the pod was big enough for only one. So, faced with the choice of either staying and dying or living and leaving, Terrill chose life. And he didn't choose Earth because he felt humans were so special. It was just that it was the closest inhabitable planet.

In fact, Terrill didn't even know about Earth until he got here, and then his advanced alien technology computer got him up to speed on what he needed to know. The most important thing, it told him, was humans like to think they're superior to all other species. Treat them as such, and you'll be fine.

Terrill was already a skilled fraudster, so playing the role of ambassador to Earth was easy. He complimented our architecture, our medicine, and our systems of government. He seemed especially enthralled with democracy, but we told him that it was becoming increasingly hard to maintain a working government when only the elderly reliably voted. The youth showed up to protest racism, the greed of evil corporations, and unfair student loan burdens, but they didn't reliably show up to cast their ballots.

This saddened Terrill, and he even agreed to participate in a voter registration drive, which, in retrospect, may have been the first humanitarian cause he had ever championed in in his life.

In retrospect, the voter participation drive was ill planned. Who thought it was a good idea to send an alien to the homes of religious nuts and racists? For some of them, who were fed their daily diet of fear from Fox News and *The Daily Caller*, every stranger was a potential invader, if not from the planet of El then from the scary border country of Mexico where each potential immigrant dreamed of taking their shitty factory jobs and their homes. Yet, many of those same haters were the first to fill their all you can eat plates at Tequila's on Taco Tuesday.

The first thirty names we crossed off on the list went okay or well enough or at least not terrible. At some houses, women said they were voting for the candidate who was a successful TV doctor. At others, frat boys didn't realize there was an election going on. Two groups of homeowners actually engaged in an informed conversation with us, though most weren't home or pretended they weren't home despite their cars being in the driveway and lights being on in the hallway.

It was house thirty-one where the incident happened. Maybe if they'd had a "No Trespassing" sign in their yard this could have been avoided. Technically, we weren't trespassing or selling anything. We were within our rights. But we were just out there to encourage active voter participation, not incite violence.

The man peeked through the curtains before opening the front door. He was dressed in a Tim Allen t-shirt, so he didn't seem too threatening at first. But, in retrospect, I should have known.

Terrill, who was canvassing for the first time, was enthusiastic. So he took the lead.

"Hi, I'm Terrill, and this is my friend Daryl," he said. "And we're from Project Get Out the Vote."

"We don't want to buy anything," the man said.

"And we're not selling anything," he said. "We just want to encourage you to vote. Democracies only function effectively when people participate in the electoral process."

I heard a woman's voice in the background. To her husband, she said, "Don, get away from the door, it's that monster from TV."

I tried to intervene to clarify, but it didn't help. "He's not a monster. He's an alien."

"You mean like those Mexicans trying to violate our borders," the man inside the house said.

I didn't know how borders, lines drawn on a map, could be violated, but I knew my saying that wouldn't help. Terrill was blond haired and blue eyed. So, I said, "Terrill's not Mexican."

"He's not even from this planet," the woman screamed. "He's from a Socialist Planet where they want to raise people's taxes and give their firstborn sons to the government."

Terrill seemed deeply disturbed, maybe in part because this description was a far cry from the reality of his planet's near-totalitarian government. Terrill seemed to realize that these people were both a lost cause and dangerous, so started walking slowly backward, as if they were bears that he wanted to quietly escape from. That was when the woman pulled out her shotgun.

"Run," I said, panicking.

Terrill slowed to a stop and started laughing. "You morons think you can hurt me with your primitive human technology. Go ahead, make my day."

Clearly, he had watched one too many Clint Eastwood movies during his brief time on Earth. I tried to shield him from the blow of the bullets, but Terrill pushed me out of the way. I landed in the grass. I watched the woman shoot him, but the bullets barely left a mark. It was like he had been bit by an annoying mosquito rather than shot by a potentially dangerous weapon.

"That's what I get from trying to do something good for once," Terrill said with disgust. "I'm not sure you humans are worth saving."

The man looked at the woman with horror. The woman looked at us with horror. They went inside and locked the door. We could still hear them screaming outside.

"Debbie, you can't just go around shooting people. They're not even armed. And they're probably Democrats. And everyone knows that Democrats are no good at winning fights, but they are good at filing lawsuits."

We were a bipartisan group, but, at this point, I don't think it was going to matter. And I definitely wasn't going to knock on their door again to clarify this minor point.

"He's not even a person," Debbie argued. "And aliens don't need weapons to kill you. They can just use that alien death grip."

Terrill stood there stunned. But I had heard enough.

"Let's go, man," I said.

"Your planet isn't more evolved," Terrill said.

"We're not," I said. "But we do have some good food here. So maybe let's just go grab a burger."

"And fries," Terrill said because he was a fan of fries.

"Sure, fries," I said. "I'm buying. You deserve a full meal after surviving a shooting."

"That thing is barely a weapon," he said.

"Our weapons keep getting stronger, faster, better. In a few years, we might make one that could kill even you."

"It's too bad that you don't make the same investment into developing your minds," he said.

"You think there's hope for the galaxy?" I asked.

"I don't know," he said. "I've only been to two planets. But it's not looking good so far. You think democracy will survive here?"

"For my lifetime at least," I said.

"Is that enough?"

"It's got to be," I said, "because it's all we have."

"If you buy a burger, I'll buy the beer," he said.

"It's a deal," I said.

"What are you doing tomorrow? I'd like to tell you about my home planet."

"Unfortunately, I'm going to be back out here knocking on doors again."

"But their bullets could kill you," he said.

"Well, maybe some things are worth dying for."

"Those idiots?" he asked.

"Well, no, but, if the rest of us vote, then maybe their candidate won't win, and then we can keep this crazy experiment in government going for another hundred years."

We walked back to my car, a Honda Civic, which I had purchased for its fuel economy.

"Your car is small," he said.

"I'm trying to save the planet."

"Good luck with that," he said.

"Thanks, I'm going to need it," I said. I let Terrill choose the music, and he picked Elton John's "Rocket Man," again. It was beginning to get tiresome. But, since he had just survived a near death experience, I didn't complain. "What's your planet like?"

"I left because they were going to kill me," he said.

"So this is just like home," I said.

"I hope not," he said as the Steve Miller Band's "Space

Cowboy" began to play.

Maybe he was fed up with the people of Earth, and if so, I didn't blame him. But, at least, I thought, he was enjoying the music.

Notes and Acknowledgements

Thank you to everyone who supported and encouraged my writing over the years including many teachers, mentors, and friends especially: Gail Adams, N.T. Arévalo, Mark Brazaitis, Sarah Beth Childers, Michael Czyzniejewski, Cara Diaconoff, Shari Goldhagen, Sarah Einstein, Catherine Cole Janonis, Heather Mercer Levine, Genevieve Marshall, Kelly Moffett, Kori Frazier Morgan, Melanie Moroz, Renee Nicholson, Claudia Putnam, Mary Ann Samyn, Emily Sartini, Natalie Sypolt, Rachel Rosolina, and Brother Tom Wendorf.

Thank you to the Hambidge Center for Creative Arts and the Elizabeth George Foundation for their early support of my writing.

Thank you to the Community of Writers for allowing me to be inspired and nurtured by their wonderful creative community.

Thank you to the AWP Writer to Writer Program for helping me get to the next step on my writing journey.

Thank you to all of the fabulous people associated with the WVU MFA program, which made me into the writer I am today, including those not listed above.

Thank you to Ariana D. Den Bleyker and ELJ Editions for pulling my manuscript out of the slush pile and making my dream of publishing a short story collection real.

Thank you also to the wonderful editors of the following literary journals in which these works first appeared, for sharing my creative vision:

"The Monsters Are Here," *Bullshit Lit.*
"Street Show Magic," *Cream Scene Carnival.*
"The Good Wolf," *Black Moon Magazine.*
"The Girl in the Mirror," *Toil & Trouble Magazine.*
"The Vampire Accountant," *Creation Magazine.*
"Hot Dog from Heaven," *Suburban Witchcraft.*
"The Expert Consultant from Amityville Gives Her Opinion on Your Second-Rate Haunted House," *Wrongturn Lit.*
"The Other Elizabeth," *Tangled Web Magazine.*
"Belonging," *Worm Moon Archive.*
"Water, Power, Danger," *Bubble Magazine.*
"Close to You," *Neuro Magazine.*
"What Remains," *JAKE.*
"Lift Me Up, Drag Me Down," *Moon City Review.*
"A Tale of Two Cats," *Kaidankai Horror Podcast.*
"Basically, Don't," *Litmora.*
"The Cold Zone," *Bright Flash Literary Magazine.*
"Under the Knife," *Worm Moon Archive.*
"The Fixer," *Fiery Scribe Review.*
"Secrets," *Idle Ink Magazine.*
"I'm Not Karen," *Cosmic Daffodil.*
"Just Like Home," *Afterpast Review.*

About the Author

Lori D'Angelo is a grant recipient from the Elizabeth George Foundation, a fellow at the Hambidge Center for Creative Arts, and an alumna of the Community of Writers. She holds an MA from Pittsburgh Theological Seminary and an MFA from West Virginia University. Her work has appeared in various literary journals including *BULL*, *Drunken Boat*, *Gargoyle*, *Moon City Review*, *Reed Magazine*, and *Rejection Letters*.